The International Traveler's Handbook

A Guide For Americans Traveling Abroad

Tom Schloetter

FW
Farwest Publishing
Issaquah, Washington

The International Traveler's Handbook
A Guide For Americans Traveling Abroad

Copyright © 1995 by Thomas Schloetter

All rights reserved. No part of this book may be reproduced, copied or transmitted in any form or by any means, electronic or mechanical, including photocopying, recording, taping, or by any information storage and retrieval system without written permission from the author, except for the inclusion of brief quotations in a review.

This book is designed to provide accurate information in regard to the subject matter covered. It is sold with the understanding that the publisher and author are not engaged in rendering legal, accounting, medical, or other professional services. If legal, accounting, medical, or other expert assistance is required, the services of a competent professional should be sought.

2nd Printing

Library of Congress Catalog No: 94-071720

ISBN: 0-9641898-0-1

Published by: Farwest Publishing
P.O. Box 1340
Issaquah, WA 98027
(206) 392-6177

Printed in the United States of America

To my wife Barb, for her love, support, and encouragement.

Acknowledgments

Many people provided information or gave assistance in the preparation of this book. To all of you—Thanks. Three people provided especially valuable assistance during this project. Special thanks to Patricia Olson for her review, copy-editing, and suggestions which greatly improved the content and clarity of many sections; to Bill Waye for his computing advice and consultation which was of tremendous assistance in producing this book and considerably improved its appearance; and especially, to my wife Barb, for helping me in every way during the writing and production of this book.

Note To Readers

The publisher and author have attempted to make this manual as complete and accurate as possible. However, with a subject as broad as international travel, specific situations or details can change quickly. Therefore, this book should be used only as a general guide and not as the ultimate source for information. Readers should always seek out other information sources, including the many sources provided in this book, in order to complement, amplify, and confirm the material in this text before planning or engaging in travel. The publisher and author shall have no liability nor responsibility to any person or entity for any damage, injury, or loss resulting from any information or advice contained in this book.

Contents

Introduction 1

Part 1 • Going Abroad

1 Passports 5
How To Apply For A U.S. Passport 6
How To Get A Passport In An Emergency 10
Obtaining Additional Visa Pages 11
Name Change 11
Loss Or Theft Of Your Passport 11
How To Obtain Two Passports For Visa Purposes 12
Passports Denied Or Revoked 13
Passport Agencies 13

2 Visas 15
Obtaining Visas 17
Visa Denials 19
Visa Violations 19
Tourist Cards 20

3 Country Entry Requirements 21
North America 22
South & Central America 22
Caribbean 24
Western Europe 27
Eastern Europe 28
Russia & The Former Soviet Union 29
Middle East & Northern Africa 30
Sub-Saharan Africa 31
Asia 33
Pacific 35

4 Arriving & Departing Foreign Countries 37
Arrivals 37
Departures 41

5 Help From American Consuls Abroad 43
When To Register With A U.S. Embassy Or Consulate 44
What U.S. Consuls Do For Americans Traveling Abroad 45
What U.S. Consuls Will Not Do For Americans Traveling Abroad 47
The Citizens Emergency Center 48

6 Money Matters 49
Foreign Currency 49
Bringing Money Abroad 51
Transferring Money Abroad From The U.S. 55
Value Added Tax (VAT) 55

7 Driving Abroad 58
Insurance 59
Driver's Licenses 60
Maps 60

8 Keeping In Touch 61
Sending Mail 61
Receiving Mail 62
Telephones 63

9 Travel Insurance 66
Types 67
Sources 68

10 Travel Safety Abroad 70
Preparing For A Safe Trip 70
Precautions While Traveling Abroad 72

11 State Department Travel Information 78
Consular Information Sheets 78
Travel Warnings 79
Free Publications From The State Department 80
State Department Publications For Sale 80

Part 2 ◆ Staying Healthy Abroad

12 Preparing For A Healthy Trip Abroad 85
What To Take 85
If You Need Medical Care Abroad 86
Health Insurance 87

13 Immunizations 89
Required Immunizations 90
Recommended Immunizations 92

14 Prevention And Precautions 95
AIDS 95
Blood Transfusions Abroad 96
Protection From Diseases Carried By Mosquitoes And Other
    Insects 97
Preventing Malaria 99
Protection From Diseases Found In Water And Beverages 101
Protection From Food-Borne Diseases 102
Travelers' Diarrhea 103
Swimming Precautions 105
Driving Injuries 105
Cruise Ship Sanitation 106
Post-Travel Illnesses 106

Part 3 ◆ Coming Home

15 U.S. Immigration & The Returning Traveler ... 109

16 Clearing U.S. Customs 111
The Declaration 111
Exemptions From Duty 113
Rates Of Duty 115
Payment Of Duty 117
GSP Duty Exemptions For Developing Countries 117
Personal Belongings Taken Abroad 120
Gifts 121

Mailing Or Shipping Items Home 121
Returning To The U.S.—Tips For Travelers 122
Obtaining Customs Assistance 123

17 Bringing Things Into The U.S. 125
Fakes 125
Duty-Free Shops 125
Money 126
Books, Recordings, Computer Programs, And Videos 126
Medicine And Narcotics 127
Firearms And Ammunition 128
Gold 128
Glazed Ceramics 129
Works Of Art 129
Antiques 129
Trademarked Items 130

18 Food, Plants, Animals, & Animal Products 131
Pets And Other Live Animals 131
Food, Plants, And Animal Products 133
Wildlife And Endangered Species Souvenirs 136

Appendices

A Documents To Take Abroad 139

B U.S. Embassies And Consulates Abroad 141

C Foreign Embassies In The U.S. 158

D Foreign Tourist Offices In The U.S. 170

E International Measurements 176

Index 178

Introduction

Millions of Americans travel overseas every year. More and more people are traveling abroad every year, many for the first time. The State Department reports that passport applications are up 17% in the first half of 1994.

For many people, international travel is one of the highlights of their lives. So many enjoy the experience because traveling abroad is so different from traveling in the U.S. It is also why international travel information is essential.

Many travelers have overseas trips that go smoothly, some have a few bumps, while a few experience disasters. Almost all travelers have some "how-to" questions about international travel. Preparations for international travel do not end after the reservations are booked. Overseas travelers are faced with a whole range of matters that must be attended to when they venture beyond the boundaries of the United States. What about passports, visas, foreign currency, customs authorities, vaccinations, health insurance, driver's licenses, or international travel safety? These topics and much more are what this book is about.

What this book is not is a guidebook to any specific city, country, or region. The language, culture, people, and places of travelers' destinations are covered in the many guidebooks of the world. But those books do not adequately address the things that all international travelers should know. Questions such as—"When do I need a visa and how do I get one?"; "What do I do if I lose my passport overseas?"; "Should I bring foreign currency from the U.S. and how do I get it?"; "When do I need immunizations?"; "How can I get help in a foreign country?"; "Can I drive overseas?"; "What can I bring back to the U.S.?"—are answered in this book.

Although travelers from other countries will find useful information inside, this handbook is specifically designed to answer the international travel questions faced by U.S. travelers. It also shows travelers how to get more information when they need it. Both seasoned and first time international travelers will find indispensable information to help them prepare before they go and travel with confidence while they are abroad. This book is also light enough to carry, so travelers can take it along and refer to it during their trips.

This book was written with one goal—to provide international travelers the information they need to have successful trips abroad. Having information about overseas travel before you go will provide peace of mind and help smooth out the bumps and prevent the disasters. With proper preparations, you can enjoy the experience of international travel instead of worrying about the details.

Do you know of other international travel information that you think would be helpful to fellow travelers? Please send your idea to the author care of Farwest Publishing, P.O. Box 1340, Issaquah, Washington, 98027. Your idea might be included in the next edition.

Have a great trip!

Part 1

Going Abroad

Part 1 provides the information you need to prepare for your trip abroad and to travel with confidence. These chapters tell you everything you need to know about passports, visas, and country entry requirements. You will learn what to expect when you arrive in or depart from a foreign country and how to get help while overseas from the U.S. Government. These chapters cover money, driving, mail, and telephones abroad. You will learn whether you need travel insurance and how to reduce your risk of becoming victimized by crime overseas. The last chapter in Part 1 tells you how to get free or cheap travel information from the U.S. State Department. With the information in these chapters, you will be well-prepared for your trip abroad.

The use of traveling is to regulate imagination by reality, and instead of thinking how things may be, to see them as they are.

—Samuel Johnson

… Chapter 1

Passports

A passport is a document issued by the government of a country which identifies the holder as a citizen of that country. It is proof of who you are and your nationality. The purpose of passports is to allow passport holders to travel across international borders. Without a passport, you cannot travel to most countries of the world or even leave the United States. With a passport, you can travel outside the U.S. and obtain the protection and services offered by U.S. diplomatic offices overseas.

Passports for Americans are issued by the U.S. State Department through the Passport Agency. Citizens of the U.S. who can prove their citizenship and identity are eligible for U.S. passports. Permanent resident aliens, those with Alien Registration Cards or *green cards,* are not U.S. citizens, and therefore, are not able to get U.S. passports.

A U.S. citizen needs a valid passport to depart from or enter the United States and to enter and depart most foreign countries. Short term travel between the United States and Canada, Mexico, and some countries in the Caribbean are exceptions. See Chapter 3, *Country Entry Requirements* to determine if you need a passport for your destination. Even if you are not required to have a passport to visit a certain country, you will need to prove your identity and citizenship before you can reenter the U.S. A passport is the best proof of citizenship, although other documents can be used.

All persons must have their own passports. Since January 1981, family members cannot be included on each other's passports.

Before traveling overseas, look at your passport to see how long it is valid. Some countries will not let you enter if your passport is valid for less than six months. Also, if you return to the United States with an expired passport, you may be charged a passport waiver fee of $100 by U.S. Immigration when you reenter the country.

It is often helpful to ensure that one or more of your family members, friends, or associates have valid passports. That way, they could travel without delay to assist you if you become seriously ill or injured or involved in some other emergency.

How To Apply For A U.S. Passport

It is a good idea to apply for your passport at least three months before you plan to travel. If you also need visas, apply earlier since you must have a valid passport before applying for a visa and obtaining visas can be time consuming (see Chapter 2). Demand for passports is heavier during certain parts of the year and processing your application may take longer during those times. Every year, demand is heaviest beginning in January and continuing until about August.

If you need a passport by a certain departure date, be sure to write your departure date on the passport application form. This block is optional, but if you do not indicate a departure date, the Passport Agency will assume that your travel plans are not immediate and will not rush the processing of your application.

You must apply in person for your first passport or when you do not meet the eligibility requirements for a passport by mail. A parent or legal guardian can apply for children under the age of 13. Passport applicants between the ages of 13 and 17 can apply on their own, but need a form of identity that teenagers often do not possess, such as a driver's license or government ID. If a teenager cannot provide proof of identity, an adult, preferably a parent or legal guardian, must appear in person with the teenager and provide proof of the adult's identity.

Applying For A Passport In Person

If you need to apply in person, you can do so at one of thirteen U.S. Passport Agency offices located in large cities, or at over 900 U.S. Post Offices or 2500 Federal and state courts or government offices that have been authorized to accept passport applications. Many telephone books list the addresses of passport acceptance facilities. Look in the Federal government listing of your phone book under *Passports*. If you cannot find a listing, contact one of the 13 Passport Agencies listed at the end of this chapter. All offices have recorded information messages that will tell where you can apply. Applying at a court or post office is often more convenient even for those people living in or near the large cities with Passport Agency offices. Passport Agencies are often very crowded and you may experience a long wait, but your passport usually is processed faster. It is often faster to complete the application at courts or post offices, but it may take longer for your passport to be delivered.

When you apply in person for your passport, you must bring five items:

1. A properly completed, but unsigned, passport application. Ask for Form DSP-11, *Passport Application*. Complete it before you present it to the passport agent, but do not sign it. You have to sign the form in the presence of the agent.

2. Proof of U.S. citizenship. There are several ways to establish proof of U.S. citizenship.

a. Previously issued passport. You can use an expired U.S. passport as proof of your U.S. citizenship. Note that if you have had a previous passport, you may be eligible to apply by mail. See below for details.

b. If you were born in the U.S. and do not have an expired U.S. passport, you need to furnish a certified copy of your birth certificate. Certified copies of birth records can be obtained from the bureau or department of vital statistics in the city, state, county, or territory where you were born. Notifications of birth registration or birth announcements are normally not accepted for passport purposes.

If you cannot obtain a birth certificate, you can submit a notice from a state registrar stating that no birth record exists. Contact the vital statistics office from the state or county that you were born for help in obtaining such a notice. Also submit as much secondary evidence of your birth as you can obtain. Examples of secondary evidence include a baptismal or circumcision certificate, hospital birth records, early census, school or family Bible records, newspaper or insurance files that note your birth, or notarized affidavits of persons having knowledge of your birth.

c. If you are a U.S. citizen who was born abroad, to prove citizenship you can use:

» A Certificate of Naturalization
» A Certificate of Citizenship
» A Report of Birth Abroad of a Citizen of the United States of America (Form FS-240)
» A Certificate of Birth (Form FS-545 or DS-1350)

d. If you do not have and cannot obtain any of these documents and are a U.S. citizen, take all available proof of your citizenship to the nearest U.S. Passport Agency and request assistance in proving your citizenship.

3. Proof of Identity. You must also establish your identity to the person accepting your application. The following items are usually accepted as proof of your identity if they contain your signature and if they readily identify you through a photograph or a physical description.

» A previous U.S. passport
» A certificate of naturalization or citizenship
» A valid driver's license
» A government (federal, state, or municipal) employee identification card
» A military identification card

These types of documents will not be accepted as proof of your identity:

» Social Security card
» Temporary or learner's driver's license
» Any temporary or expired identity card
» Any document that has been altered or changed in any way

If you are unable to present any of the acceptable documents to prove your identity, you can apply for your passport accompanied by a person who has known you for at least two years and who is a U.S. citizen or a permanent resident alien. That person must be willing to attest to your identity. In this situation, also submit any other proof of identification that you possess.

4. Photographs. You must submit two identical photographs of yourself taken within the past 6 months. The photographs must be 2 x 2 inches in size. They can be either black and white or color.

The photos must be a good likeness of you. The Passport Agency recommends photographs where you are relaxed and smiling. Photographs must be front view, full-face, portrait-type prints taken of you in normal street attire without a hat. No more than your head and shoulders or upper torso may be shown. Dark glasses may not be worn unless you wear them for medical reasons. You can wear a head covering only if worn for religious reasons. Vending machine photographs are not accepted.

The easiest way to obtain acceptable photographs is to have them taken at a location that regularly produces passport photos. Many photography studios, quick photo processing shops, copy shops, and automobile club offices have the camera equipment needed to produce identical passport photos. You can find passport photo locations in the yellow pages of your phone book under *Passport and Visa Services*.

5. The correct fee. The passport fee for applicants over the age of 18 is currently $65. The Passport Agency says the fee is $55 plus a $10 execution fee, but it still comes to $65 to get a passport. The passport will be valid for 10 years from the date of issuance. Passports for applicants under the age of 18 currently cost $40 and are valid for 5 years.

You can pay for your passport by check—personal, certified, traveler's, bank draft, or cashier's—or by money order. You can also pay by cash at a Passport Agency, but not at all post offices, courts, or government offices. Credit cards are not accepted for payment of the passport fee.

Applying For A Passport By Mail

You may be eligible to obtain your passport by mail. You can get your passport by mail if **all** the following apply to you:

» You were issued a passport within 12 years of the time of your new application.
» You can submit your most recent passport with your new application.
» Your previous passport was issued on or after your 18th birthday.
» You use the same name as that on your most recent passport or you have had your name changed by marriage or court order.

To obtain your passport by mail, request Form DSP-82, *Application for Passport By Mail*, from one of the offices that accepts passport applications or from your travel agent. Complete the application including signing and dating the form. Submit the application to the National Passport Center at the address on the form. Do not submit an application by mail to a local Passport Agency office or other passport acceptance facility. You must enclose your previous passport, two identical photographs (see previous section), and the correct fee of $55. The fee is payable by check or money order made out to "Passport Services." Your full name and date of birth must be typed or printed on the front of the check or money order. If your name has changed also submit the original or certified copy of the court order or marriage certificate that shows your name change. The name change document must bear an official seal. After you submit your passport application by mail, you can check on its status by calling (603) 334-0500.

When you receive your passport by mail, sign it right away. Your previous passport and the original documents you submitted will be returned to you with your new passport.

How To Get A Passport In An Emergency

The Passport Agencies can quickly issue a passport in cases of genuine, documented emergencies. You will need to provide proof that your travel is necessary and imminent such as showing your airline tickets or some documentation of the emergency. You can apply for an emergency passport at any passport acceptance facility and pay to have your passport delivered by express mail. However, for faster processing the Passport Agency recommends that you apply for an emergency passport at one of the Passport Agency offices. It is best to call ahead, discuss your specific situation, and ask the Passport Agency exactly what they need as proof that you have a genuine emergency requiring the issuance of an expedited passport.

Obtaining Additional Visa Pages

You will need many visa pages if you often travel to countries that require visas. When you need additional visa pages before your passport expires, obtain them by sending your passport to one of the Passport Agencies. You do not need to apply in person. Complete Form DSP-19, *Passport Amendment/Validation Application*, available from any of the offices that accept passport applications. Under the "Other Action Requested" section, write "Visa Supplement Pages." If you travel frequently to countries requiring visas, you can request a 48 page passport at the time you apply for your passport. There is no additional charge for the extra visa pages or for the 48 page passport.

Name Change

If you have changed your name, you will need to amend your passport. To do so use DSP-19, *Passport Amendment/Validation Application*. Submit this form along with proof of your name change such as a marriage certificate, divorce decree, or certified court order to the nearest Passport Agency office. You do not need to appear in person. There is no fee to have your passport amended.

Loss Or Theft Of Your Passport

Your passport is your most important travel document. Protect it. Its loss could cause you unnecessary travel complications and expenses.

If your passport is lost or stolen in the United States report its loss immediately to the nearest Passport Agency or to Passport Services, Department of State, 1425 K Street NW, Washington D.C. 20524.

If your passport is lost or stolen abroad, report its loss immediately to the local police. Get a copy of the report and present it to the nearest U.S. Embassy or Consulate. See Appendix B for the locations of U.S. Embassies and Consulates. The embassy or consulate will likely ask you for a written statement explaining how your passport was lost or stolen and what you have done to try to recover it. You will need to complete a new application, provide passport photos and pay the passport fee again. Consider carrying extra passport photos when you travel abroad to help speed the process should you need a replacement passport.

It can take several hours to several days to replace a lost or stolen passport overseas. The processing time will depend on what kind of proof of identity and citizenship you can provide. The better the proof, the quicker the passport. If you can provide the consular officer with the information contained in your passport, it will make it much easier for you to obtain a new passport. Photocopy the first two pages of your passport (the pages with your signature and picture). Keep the copies with you when you travel abroad but in a place separate from your passport. Replacing your passport will also be easier if you carry a copy of your birth certificate. It is a good idea to leave your passport number, date, and place of issuance with a relative or friend in the United States who could provide you the information by phone if you were to lose everything abroad.

Some travelers keep their expired passports to take along on their international trips. An expired passport is excellent proof that you are a U.S. citizen and are eligible for a replacement passport.

How To Obtain Two Passports For Visa Purposes

Some countries will not issue you a visa if your passport shows that you have traveled to certain countries. The most notable example is Americans who travel to the Middle East cannot obtain visas for many Arab countries if their passports show travel to Israel. To help Americans in these situations, the State Department will issue a second passport, valid for two years, so that travelers can have visa stamps placed in separate passports. To obtain a limited-duration second passport go to a Passport Agency or U.S. Embassy or Consulate and submit:

» A valid passport
» A completed passport application
» Two passport photos
» The passport fee
» A written request for a second passport for the purpose of obtaining visas.
» A statement that if either passport is lost you will report the loss to the nearest U.S. Embassy, Consulate, or Passport Agency.

Passports Denied Or Revoked

The Passport Agency can deny a passport application or revoke a previously issued passport. Usually this is done to prevent an individual from leaving the country. Reasons for denying or revoking passports include when an individual has an outstanding arrest warrant, a probation order disallowing travel abroad, a psychiatric commitment order, or a pending extradition request.

Passport Agencies

Boston Passport Agency
Thomas P. O'Neill Federal Bldg.
10 Causeway Street, Room 247
Boston Massachusetts 02222
Recording: (617) 565-6698
Public Inquiries: (617) 565-6990

Chicago Passport Agency
Kluczynski Federal Building
230 South Dearborn St., Suite 380
Chicago, Illinois 60604
Recording: (312) 353-5426
Public Inquiries: (312) 353-7155

Honolulu Passport Agency
New Federal Building
300 Ala Moana Blvd., Room C-106
Honolulu, Hawaii 96850
Recording: (808) 541-1919
Public Inquiries: (808) 541-1918

Houston Passport Agency
Mickey Leland Federal Building
1919 Smith Street, Suite 1100
Houston, Texas 77002
Recording: (713) 653-3159
Public Inquiries: (713) 653-3153

14 The International Traveler's Handbook

Los Angeles Passport Agency
11000 Wilshire Blvd., Room 13100
Los Angeles, California 90024
Recording: (310) 575-7070
Public Inquiries: (310) 575-7075

Miami Passport Agency
Federal Office Building
51 Southwest First Ave., 3rd Fl.
Miami, Florida 33130
Recording: (305) 536-4681 (English or Spanish)
Public Inquiries: (305) 536-4681

New Orleans Passport Agency
Postal Services Building
701 Loyola Ave., Room T-12005
New Orleans, Louisiana 70113
Recording: (504) 589-6728
Public Inquiries: (504) 589-6161

New York Passport Agency
Rockefeller Center
630 Fifth Avenue, Room 270
New York, NY 10111
Recording: (212) 399-5290
Public Inquiries: (212) 399-7710

Philadelphia Passport Agency
Federal Building
600 Arch Street, Room 4426
Philadelphia, Pennsylvania 19106
Recording: (215) 597-7480
Public Inquiries: (215) 597-7480

San Francisco Passport Agency
Tishman Speyer Building
525 Market Street, Suite 200
San Francisco, California 94105
Recording: (415) 744-4444
Public Inquiries: (415) 744-4010

Seattle Passport Agency
Federal Office Building
915 Second Avenue, Room 992
Seattle, Washington 98174
Recording: (206) 220-7777
Public Inquiries: (206) 220-7788

Stamford Passport Agency
One Landmark Square
Broad and Atlantic Streets
Stamford, Connecticut 06901
Recording: (203) 325-4401
Public Inquiries: (203) 325-3538

Washington Passport Agency
1425 K Street NW
Washington, D.C. 20524
Recording: (202) 647-0518
Public Inquiries: (202) 647-0518

The telephone numbers shown above as recordings operate 24 hours a day. They provide recorded messages concerning general passport information, Passport Agency locations, hours of operation, and how to obtain emergency passport services during nonworking hours.

Chapter 2

Visas

A visa is official permission to visit a country issued to an individual who requests to travel there. It is simply a stamp or endorsement placed in your passport (or sometimes on a separate sheet) by an official of a foreign country. It shows that your passport and visa application have been reviewed and that you meet the requirements for entry into the country. A visa permits you to visit that country for a limited period of time and for a specific purpose. For example, a country you wish to visit may issue you a 90 day tourist visa, meaning that your visit to that country can last up to 90 days for purposes of touring the country only. This type of visa would not allow you to conduct any business or become a student during your visit. Most countries charge a fee for issuing the visa. Fees are usually in the $15-$50 range.

There are four basic kinds of visas: tourist, business, student, and resident. Most international travelers will only be concerned with tourist visas and this chapter focuses on that type. However, much of this information is also applicable to the other kinds of visas. If you need a visa other than a tourist visa, be sure you start the application process well in advance of your trip. Countries usually require that travelers submit more extensive documentation for other kinds of visas.

You obtain visas from the embassy or consulate of the countries you wish to visit. **Visas for U.S. citizens are issued by foreign governments, not the U.S. Government.** Neither U.S. Passport Agencies nor the State Department can help you obtain visas. Almost every country with diplomatic relations with the U.S. has an embassy in Washington, D.C. that will issue visas through their consular section. In addition, countries with strong ties to the U.S. often maintain foreign consular offices in one or more major U.S. cities. Appendix C lists the addresses and phone numbers of foreign embassies in the U.S. Also look in your city's telephone book under *Consulates & Foreign Country Representatives* to see if there is a foreign consular office nearby of the country you wish to visit.

It is not necessary for Americans to hold visas to enter the majority of the countries of the world. Approximately 45% of countries require that U.S. citizens hold visas to enter for normal tourist travel. Several others require a visa for those traveling on business. To enter many countries, U.S. visitors need only hold a passport. For some countries such as Mexico, travelers need a tourist card instead of a visa. Canada does not require U.s. citizens to have either a passport or visa to enter. Generally, countries in Europe, the Caribbean, Japan, and most Latin American countries do not require visas of U.S. citizens for normal tourist visits. You will usually need a visa for longer stays or non-tourist travel in those countries or for travel to most other countries for any purpose.

Before embarking on an overseas trip, find out whether the countries you want to visit require that you hold a visa to enter. Chapter 3 shows the entry requirements for every country. If possible, you should obtain visas before you leave the United States. In some countries, if you arrive without the necessary visa, you will not be able to obtain a visa in the country and will be denied entry.

Visas are issued as either single entry or multiple entry. A multiple entry visa allows you to enter, leave, and reenter a country several times. This kind of visa is especially useful if you plan to use one country as your base to visit several other countries. Visas also must be used within a specified period of time after they are issued. The time of visa validity varies from country to country. While it is good to get your visas well in advance of your trip, be sure your visas are still valid when you travel.

Obtaining Visas

There are at least five ways to obtain a visa should your travels require one. The method you choose will usually depend on how much time you have to obtain visas before your trip.

In person or by mail. Probably the most common method, individuals apply directly to the country they want to visit. Call, write, or visit the foreign embassy in Washington, D.C., a nearby consulate, or the country's tourist office. See Appendices C and D for addresses and phone numbers. Request the country's current entry requirements and visa forms. Complete the application and submit it, the required fee and photos, and your passport. You passport and the visa (if approved) will be returned to you by mail or held for pick up.

Through travel agencies and tour operators. If you used a travel agent or tour operator to arrange your trip, they may also assist you in obtaining any necessary visas. Some tour operators make all the visa arrangements for the tour participants. At the least, travel agents and tour operators should be able to tell you whether you need visas for the countries you will visit and where to write for visa information and applications.

Through visa services. Located in Washington, D.C. and in many large cities are companies that will obtain the necessary visas for you for a fee. Visa service companies should have the current entry requirements and the necessary forms for all countries. The charge for a visa obtained through a visa service is about $35-$50 per visa plus the visa fee charged by the foreign embassy. To locate a visa service in your area, look in your yellow pages under *Passport and Visa Services*.

Upon Arrival. Resort to obtaining a visa on arrival only in emergencies or only when the embassy or consulate has advised you that this is an acceptable practice. Some countries will permit you to do this while others will not. Even in those countries that issue visas at ports of entry, you may arrive when the visa office is closed and be forced to wait until it reopens before being admitted to the country. Visas-on-the-spot are usually only available at major airports, not normally at border crossings. You may also find that airlines will not allow you on the plane at your departure point if you do not have the necessary visa.

In Neighboring Countries. You may be able to obtain visas for the country you wish to visit while you are in a neighboring country. This approach is especially recommended if you were unable to obtain the visa while in the U.S. You may find that the visa issuing standards are more relaxed in neighboring countries than they were in the U.S. Make sure that you carry extra passport photos if you will attempt to get visas while abroad.

If at all possible, especially if you know your itinerary, try to obtain required visas before you depart. You are traveling to see the country, not wait in a long line at a foreign embassy or immigration office. You can easily lose one or more days obtaining a visa. Also, if you apply for a visa in the U.S., you complete the application in English. If you file for a visa overseas, you will probably be required to have your application translated to another language. This adds both time and expense to the visa process.

Visa Applications

To obtain a visa you will have to complete a form and provide information on yourself and your planned trip. You normally will submit one or more photographs of yourself. Many countries require a fee for issuing a visa. When applying for visas, be sure that your passport contains enough visa pages. The visa stamp for some countries will cover both the left and right hand sides of passport pages. Because a visa is stamped directly onto a blank page in your passport, you will need to give or mail your passport to an official of each foreign embassy or consulate of the countries you plan to visit. This means that you can apply for only one visa at a time. Therefore, obtaining several visas through the mail can be a time consuming process. Just getting the necessary visa application form from some countries can be difficult.

Allow sufficient time prior to your departure for processing your visa application, especially if you are applying by mail. Because visa processing times for different countries vary so much, it is impossible to give an accurate estimate of the time required. It could be days or it could be weeks. The best advice is to start early. You may be able to obtain a second passport if you need several visas but have little time to obtain them, or if you need to travel after your passport has been submitted to a foreign embassy for visa processing. Contact a U.S. Passport Agency.

Visa Denials

Visa applications can be denied. The most common reason for a visa denial is that your application was not in order—you did not submit proper photographs or the correct fee, or fill out the application correctly. Visa applications may seem picky, tedious, and bureaucratic. They are, but if you do not follow the application rules, you probably will not get the visa until you submit a correct application. Save yourself the grief and do it right the first time.

Other reasons visas may be denied:

» Previous travel to "incompatible" countries. If your passport shows visa or airport arrival stamps for travel to certain countries, other countries may not give you a visa. Many Arab countries will not issue you a visa if your passport shows Israeli visa stamps. Some African countries have denied visas if passports showed previous travel to South Africa. The only solution is to obtain a new passport that does not contain visa stamps showing travel to those countries. The State Department will issue limited duration second passports for this purpose. Refer to Chapter 1, *Passports*, for more information.

» Incompatible Political Beliefs. This is a rare occurrence and would happen only if the country you wish to visit believes that your presence or planned activities in the country would be disruptive.

» Incompatible Religious Beliefs. Also rare. Some countries may still deny a visa if they oppose your religious beliefs.

Visa Violations

Remember, visas are permission for you to enter and visit a country for a limited time and for a specific purpose. The length of time you can stay is stamped on the visa in your passport. Even countries that do not require a visa for a limited stay, such as a 90 day visit, will require that you get one if your stay extends beyond the time limit. If you are still in a country and your visa will expire before you leave, try to get it extended **before** it expires. If you cannot get an extension, try to obtain resident status. If you cannot get a visa extension or resident status, you should leave the country. Remaining in the country with an expired visa makes you an illegal alien. If your visa expires and you are still in the country, depending on the country, you could be fined and deported, have difficulties leaving the country, or even be arrested.

In most countries, you can get an extension of stay fairly routinely if you apply before your stay expires. If you have overstayed your visit, getting a visa extension is no longer routine. To get an extension you normally must apply in person with the country's immigration authorities. Many countries will also require that you register with the local police when extending your stay.

Tourist Cards

Some countries only require that you hold a tourist card instead of a visa to gain entry. A tourist card is similar to a visa, but simpler to obtain. The cards permit travel to a country for a specific period of time and are used for short term visitors. Many Latin American and Caribbean countries require tourist cards, not visas, for U.S. citizens. You can obtain a tourist card from the country's embassy, consulate, or tourist office, from an airline serving the country, or at the port of entry. You will need some proof of citizenship such as a passport, birth certificate, or voter's registration card. A fee sometimes is charged for tourist cards.

Chapter 3

Country Entry Requirements

This chapter contains the entry requirements for all countries of the world for U.S. citizens traveling as tourists or on business. Entry requirements are the same for tourist and business travelers unless specifically stated. The entry requirements are arranged by region. This information was current at the time of printing, but can change. Check the entry requirements with the embassy or consulate of each country you plan to visit before going abroad, especially if you will be traveling in Africa, the Middle East, Asia, or Eastern Europe. Appendix C contains the addresses and phone numbers of all foreign embassies in the United States.

Some countries require an *onward/return ticket* or *proof of sufficient funds* for entry. Onward/return ticket means that you will have to produce proof when you enter that you will leave the country, usually in the form of a transportation ticket. If your plans are such that you do not have a ticket, some countries with this requirement will require that you place money on deposit to cover the cost of a ticket. Proof of sufficient funds means that you will have to show on entry that you have enough money to pay for your stay. The amount varies by country and the length of stay.

While entry requirements vary country to country, all countries will require that you be able to identify yourself. You will also need proof of your identity when you reenter the U.S. When traveling abroad, always carry your driver's license or other form of ID.

The United States has restricted travel by Americans to certain countries and U.S. passports are not valid for travel to those countries. In some cases the State Department will permit Americans to travel to restricted countries by issuing a special passport validation. If a country listing below shows that travel is restricted, contact the State Department's Passport Services for information on applying for a special passport validation. The address and phone number are: Deputy Assistant Secretary for Passport Services, U.S. Department of State, 1425 K Street, NW, Washington, D.C., 20522-1705, Attention: Office of Citizenship Appeals and Legal Assistance, Room 300; (202) 326-6168.

North America

Canada—Proof of U.S. citizenship and photo ID required. No visa required for tourists entering from the U.S. for a stay up to 180 days. A Minister's Permit is required for anyone with a criminal record (including a DWI charge). U.S. citizens entering Canada from a third country must have a valid passport.

Mexico—No passport or visa required for tourist stay up to 90 days. A tourist card is required, valid for a single trip up to 180 days. Tourist cards can be obtained in advance from a consulate, tourism office, and most airlines serving Mexico. Business travelers need a passport and visa.

South & Central America

Argentina—Passport required. No visa required for tourist stay up to 90 days. Business travelers need a passport and visa.

Belize—Passport, return/onward ticket, and sufficient funds required. No visa required for stay up to 1 month.

Bolivia—Passport required. No visa required for tourist stay up to 30 days. Business travelers need a passport and visa.

Brazil—Tourists need a passport and visa. Visa must be obtained in advance. For business travelers conducting only business discussions, a tourist visa is sufficient, otherwise a business visa is required.

Chile—Passport required. No visa required for stay up to 90 days. Tourist card required; issued on arrival.

Columbia—Passport, proof of onward/return ticket, and entry permit required for stay up to 90 days. Entry permits are issued at the port of entry.

Costa Rica—Passport required. Travelers are sometimes admitted with original certified U.S. birth certificate and photo ID for tourist stay up to 90 days. Tourist card issued upon arrival at airport. U.S. citizens must have onward/return ticket.

Ecuador—Passport and return/onward ticket required for stays up to 90 days.

El Salvador—Passport and visa required. Visa can be valid up to 90 days, but length of stay is determined by immigration authorities upon arrival. Obtain visa in advance.

French Guiana—Proof of U.S. citizenship and photo ID required for visit up to 3 weeks. For stays longer than 3 weeks a passport is required.

Galapagos Islands—Passport and onward/return ticket required.

Guatemala—Passport and tourist card or visa required. Tourist card issued by consulate or airline serving Guatemala. Requires proof of U.S. citizenship and photo ID. Length of stay for the visa and tourist card is determined upon arrival.

Guyana—Passport and visa required. Single entry tourist visa is valid for stay up to 90 days.

Honduras—Passport and onward/return ticket required.

Nicaragua—Passport, valid 6 months beyond duration of stay, is required. Onward/return ticket and sufficient funds ($200 minimum) are required.

Panama—Proof of U.S. citizenship and tourist card required for passengers arriving by commercial carrier. Tourist card is available on arrival or from airlines serving Panama. For longer stays or for travelers arriving by private plane, car, or boat, a passport and visa are required.

Paraguay—Passport required. No visa required for stay up to 90 days.

Peru—Passport required. No visa required for tourist stay up to 90 days. Tourists may need onward/return ticket. Business travelers need a passport and visa.

Suriname—Passport and visa required.

Uruguay—Passport required. No visa required for stay up to 90 days.

Venezuela—Tourists need passport and tourist card. Tourist card can be obtained from airlines serving Venezuela. Valid for 60 days and cannot be extended. Multiple entry visa valid up to one year should be obtained for longer stays. Business travelers need a passport and visa.

Caribbean

Antigua and Barbuda—Proof of U.S. citizenship required. Return/onward ticket and/or proof of sufficient funds needed for tourist stay up to 6 months.

Aruba—Passport or proof of U.S. citizenship required. No visa required for stay up to 14 days. Proof of onward/return ticket or sufficient funds for stay may be required.

Bahamas—Proof of U.S. citizenship, photo ID and onward/return ticket required for stay up to 8 months.

Barbados—U.S. citizens traveling directly from the U.S. to Barbados may enter for up to 90 days with proof of U.S. citizenship, photo ID, and onward/return ticket. Passport required for longer visits. Business travelers need a passport and visa for financial transactions.

Bermuda—Proof of U.S. citizenship, photo ID, and onward/return ticket for tourist stay up to 21 days.

Bonaire—See Netherlands Antilles.

Cayman Islands—See West Indies, British.

Cuba—U.S. citizens need a U.S. Treasury Department license to engage in any transactions related to travel within Cuba. Contact the Licensing Division, Office of Foreign Assets Control, Dept. of Treasury, 1331 G St. NW, Washington, D.C. 20220, (202) 622-2480. If a license is granted, a passport and visa are required.

Curacao—See Netherlands Antilles.

Dominica—Proof of U.S. citizenship, photo ID, and onward/return ticket required for tourist stay up to 6 months. For longer stays, contact embassy.

Dominican Republic—Passport or proof of U.S. citizenship and tourist card or visa required. Tourist card for stay up to 60 days available from embassy or from airline serving the country. Obtain visa for longer stays.

Grenada—Passport recommended. May enter with proof of U.S. citizenship and photo ID. No visa required for stay up to 90 days.

Guadeloupe—See West Indies, French.

Haiti—Passport required.

Jamaica—If traveling directly from the U.S., Puerto Rico, or the U.S. Virgin Islands, U.S. citizens need an onward/return ticket, proof of U.S. citizenship, photo ID, and proof of sufficient funds. Tourist card issued on arrival for stay up to 6 months. Business travelers need a passport and visa.

Leeward Islands—See Virgin Islands, British.

Martinique—See West Indies, French.

Netherland Antilles—Includes the islands of Bonaire, Curacao, Saba, Statia, St. Maarten. Passport or proof of U.S. citizenship required.

No visa required for stays up to 14 days. Stay can be extended after arrival. Tourists may be required to show onward/return ticket or proof of sufficient funds for stay.

Nevis—See Saint Kitts and Nevis.

Saba—See Netherlands Antilles.

Saint Kitts and Nevis—Proof of U.S. citizenship, photo ID, and onward/return ticket required for stay up to 6 months.

Saint Lucia—Passport (or proof of U.S. citizenship and photo ID) and onward/return ticket required for stay up to 6 months.

St. Martin—See West Indies, French.

St. Maarten—See Netherlands Antilles.

Saint Vincent and the Grenadines—Proof of U.S. citizenship, photo ID, and onward/return ticket or proof of sufficient funds required for tourist stay up to 6 months.

Trinidad and Tobago—Passport required. No visa required for stay up to 2 months.

Turks and Caicos—See West Indies, British.

Virgin Islands, British—Includes islands of Anegarda, Jost van Dyke, Tortola, and Virgin Gorda. Proof of U.S. citizenship, photo ID, onward/return ticket, and sufficient funds required for stay up to 90 days.

West Indies, British—Includes islands of Anguilla, Montserrat, Cayman Islands, Turks and Caicos. Proof of U.S. citizenship, photo ID, onward/return ticket, and sufficient funds required for tourist stay up to 90 days.

West Indies, French—Includes islands of Guadeloupe, Isles des Saintes, La Desirade, Marie Galante, Saint Barthelemy, St. Martin, and Martinique. Proof of U.S. citizenship and photo ID required for visit up to 3 weeks. For longer stays a passport is required. No visa is required for stays up to 90 days.

Western Europe

Andorra—See France.

Austria—Passport required. No visa required for stay up to 90 days.

Belgium—Passport required. No visa required for stay up to 90 days.

Denmark—Passport required. No visa required for stay up to 90 days. Note that the 3 month period begins when entering any Scandinavian country: Denmark, Finland, Iceland, Norway, Sweden.

England—See United Kingdom.

Finland—Passport required. No visa required for stay up to 90 days. Note that the 3 month period begins when entering any Scandinavian country: Denmark, Finland, Iceland, Norway, Sweden.

France—Passport required to visit France, Andorra, Monaco, and Corsica. No visa required for stay up to 90 days.

Germany—Passport required. No visa required for stay up to 90 days.

Gibraltar—Passport required. No visa required for stay up to 90 days.

Greece—Passport required. No visa required for stay up to 90 days.

Iceland—Passport required. No visa required for stay up to 90 days. Note that the 3 month period begins when entering any Scandinavian country: Denmark, Finland, Iceland, Norway, Sweden.

Ireland—Passport required. No visa required for stay up to 90 days.

Italy—Passport required. No visa required for stay up to 90 days.

Liechtenstein—Passport required. No visa required for stay up to 90 days.

Luxembourg—Passport required. No visa required for stay up to 90 days.

Malta—Passport required. No visa required for stay up to 90 days.

Monaco—Passport required. No visa required for stay up to 90 days.

Netherlands—Passport required. No visa required for stay up to 90 days.

Norway—Passport required. No visa required for stay up to 90 days. Note that the 3 month period begins when entering any Scandinavian country: Denmark, Finland, Iceland, Norway, Sweden.

Portugal—Passport required. No visa required for stay up to 60 days.

San Marino—Passport required. No visa required for stay up to 90 days.

Scotland—See United Kingdom.

Spain—Passport required. No visa required for stay up to 6 months.

Sweden—Passport required. No visa required for stay up to 90 days. Note that the 3 month period begins when entering any Scandinavian country: Denmark, Finland, Iceland, Norway, Sweden.

Switzerland—Passport required. No visa required for stay up to 90 days.

United Kingdom (England, Northern Ireland, Scotland & Wales)—Passport required. No visa required for stay up to 6 months.

Vatican—Passport required. No visa required for stay up to 90 days.

Eastern Europe

Albania—Passport and visa required.

Bulgaria—Passport required. No visa required for stay up to 30 days.

Croatia—Passport and visa required.

Czech Republic—Passport required. No visa required for stay up to 30 days.

Hungary—Passport required. No visa required for stay up to 90 days.

Poland—Passport required. No visa required for stay up to 90 days. Visitors must register at hotel or with police within 48 hours of arrival.

Romania—Passport and visa required.

Serbia and Montenegro—Passport and visa required.

Slovak Republic—Passport required. No visa required for stay up to 30 days.

Slovenia—Passport required. No visa required for stay up to 90 days.

Russia & The Former Soviet Union

Armenia—Passport and visa required.

Azerbaijan—Passport and visa required.

Belarus—Passport and visa required.

Estonia—Passport required. No visa required for stay up to 90 days.

Georgia—Passport and visa required.

Kazakhstan—Passport and visa required.

Kyrgyzstan—Passport and visa required.

Latvia—Passport and visa required.

Lithuania—Passport and visa required.

Moldova—Passport and visa required.

Russia—Passport and visa required.

Tajikistan—Passport and visa required.

Turkmenistan—Passport and visa required.

Ukraine—Passport and visa required.

Uzbekistan—Passport and visa required.

Middle East & Northern Africa

Algeria—Passport and visa required. Proof of onward/return ticket and sufficient funds needed to obtain visa. Visa not granted if passport shows travel to Israel.

Bahrain—Passport and visa required. No tourist visas are currently being issued. Transit visas for a stay of 72 hours issued on arrival. Travelers with passports showing travel to Israel will be delayed or denied entry.

Cyprus—Passport required. No visa required for stay up to 90 days.

Egypt—Passport and visa required.

Iran—Passport and visa required. The U.S. does not maintain diplomatic relations with Iran. Contact the Embassy of Pakistan.

Iraq—The U.S. does not permit tourist or business travel to Iraq at this time.

Israel—Passport, onward/return ticket, and proof of sufficient funds required. No visa required for stay up to 90 days.

Jordan—Passport and visa required. Travelers with passports showing travel to Israel may be denied entry.

Kuwait—Passport and visa required.

Lebanon—The U.S. does not permit travel to Lebanon except in rare circumstances. Contact Passport Services at the Department of State for information.

Libya—The U.S. does not permit travel to Libya except in rare circumstances. Contact Passport Services at the Department of State for information.

Morocco—Passport required. No visa required for stay up to 90 days.

Oman—Passport and visa required. Visa not granted if passport shows travel to Israel.

Qatar—Passport and visa required. Visa not granted if passport shows travel to Israel.

Saudi Arabia—Tourist travel is not permitted. Business travelers need a passport and visa.

Syria—Passport and visa required. Visa not granted if passport shows travel to Israel.

Tunisia—Passport and onward/return ticket required. No visa required for stay up to 4 months.

Turkey—Passport required. No visa required for stay up to 90 days.

United Arab Emirates—Passport and visa required.

Yemen—Passport and visa required. Travelers with passports showing travel to South Africa or Israel will be denied visas.

Sub-Saharan Africa

Angola—Tourist travel is not permitted. Business travelers need a passport and visa. Travelers with passports showing travel to South Africa may be denied visas.

Benin—Passport and visa required.

Botswana—Passport required. No visa required for stay up to 90 days.

Burkina Faso—Passport and visa required.

Burundi—Passport and visa required.

Cameroon—Passport and visa required.

Cape Verde—Passport and visa required.

Central African Republic—Passport and visa required.

Chad—Passport and visa required.

Comoros Islands—Passport, onward/return ticket, and visa required.

Congo—Passport and visa required.

Cote D'Ivoire—Passport required. No visa required for stay up to 90 days.

Djibouti—Passport and visa required.

Equatorial Guinea—Passport and visa required.

Eritrea—Passport and travel permit required.

Ethiopia—Passport and visa required.

Gabon—Passport and visa required.

Gambia—Passport and visa required.

Ghana—Passport and visa required.

Guinea—Passport and visa required.

Guinea-Bissau—Passport and visa required.

Kenya—Passport and visa required.

Lesotho—Passport and visa required.

Liberia—Passport and visa required.

Madagascar—Passport and visa required.

Malawi—Passport required. No visa required for stay up to 1 year.

Mali—Passport and visa required.

Mauritania—Passport and visa required.

Mauritius—Passport, sufficient funds, and onward/return ticket required. No visa required for stay up to 90 days.

Mozambique—Passport and visa required.

Namibia—Passport, onward/return ticket, and proof of sufficient funds required. No visa required for stay up to 90 days. Travelers with passports showing travel to South Africa may be denied entry.

Niger—Passport and visa required.

Nigeria—Passport and visa required.

Rwanda—Passport and visa required.

Sao Tome and Principe—Passport and visa required.

Senegal—Passport required. No visa required for stay up to 90 days.

Seychelles—Passport, onward/return ticket, and proof of sufficient funds required. Visa issued on arrival.

Sierra Leone—Passport and visa required.

Somalia—Contact the Somali Consulate in New York (212) 688-9410) for current entry information.

South Africa—Passport required. No visa required for stay up to 90 days.

Sudan—Passport and visa required.

Swaziland—Passport required. No visa required for stay up to 60 days.

Tanzania—Passport and visa required.

Togo—Passport required. No visa required for stay up to 90 days.

Uganda—Passport required. No visa required for stay up to 90 days.

Zaire—Passport and visa required.

Zambia—Passport and visa required.

Zimbabwe—Passport, onward/return ticket, and proof of sufficient funds required. No visa required for stay up to 90 days.

Asia

Afghanistan—Tourist travel is not permitted. Business travelers need a passport and visa.

Bangladesh—Passport, visa, and onward/return ticket required.

Bhutan—Passport and visa required. Tourist visas issued only to members of organized tours.

Brunei—Passport and visa required.

Cambodia—Passport and visa required.

China, People's Republic of—Passport and visa required.

Hong Kong—Passport and onward/return ticket required. No visa required for stay up to 30 days.

India—Passport and visa required.

Indonesia—Passport and onward/return ticket required. No visa required for stay up to 60 days.

Japan—Passport and onward/return ticket required. No visa required for stay up to 90 days.

Korea, North—Tourist travel is not permitted. Business travelers need a passport, visa, and a U.S. Treasury Department license to engage in any transactions with North Korea. Contact the Licensing Division, Office of Foreign Assets Control, Dept. of Treasury, 1331 G St. NW, Washington, D.C. 20220, (202) 622-2480.

Korea, South—Passport required. No visa required for stay up to 15 days. Business travelers need a passport and visa.

Laos—Passport and visa required. Tourist visas issued only to members of organized tours.

Macau—Passport required. No visa required for stay up to 60 days.

Malaysia—Passport required. No visa required for stay up to 90 days.

Maldives—Passport onward/return ticket, and sufficient funds required. Visa issued on arrival.

Mongolia—Passport and visa required.

Myanmar (Burma)—Passport and visa required.

Nepal—Passport and visa required.

Pakistan—Passport and visa required.

Philippines—Passport and onward/return ticket required. No visa required for tourist stay up to 21 days. Business travelers need a visa.

Singapore—Passport and onward/return ticket required. No visa required for stay up to 14 days, can be extended to 3 months.

Sri Lanka—Passport, onward/return ticket, and proof of sufficient funds required. Tourists need no visa for stays up to 30 days. Business travelers need a passport and visa.

Taiwan—Passport required. No visa required for stay up to 5 days. Visa required for longer stays.

Thailand—Passport and onward/return ticket required. Tourists need no visa for stays up to 15 days if arriving and departing from a Thai international airport. Visa required for longer stays. Business travelers need a passport and visa.

Vietnam—Passport and visa required.

Pacific

Australia—Passport, visa, and onward/return ticket required.

Cook Islands—Passport and onward/return ticket required. No visa required for stay up to 31 days.

Fiji—Passport, onward/return ticket, and proof of sufficient funds required. Visa issued on arrival.

French Polynesia—Includes Tahiti, Society Islands, Tuamotu, Gambier, French Austral, Marquesas, Kerguelen, Crozet, New Caledonia, Wallis, and Fortuna Islands. Passport required. No visa required for stay up to 30 days.

Kiribati—(Formerly Gilbert Islands) Passport and visa required.

Marshall Islands—Proof of U.S. citizenship, sufficient funds for stay, and onward/return ticket required.

Micronesia—Proof of U.S. citizenship, sufficient funds for stay and onward/return ticket required.

Nauru—Passport and onward/return ticket required. Visa required for stay longer than 3 days.

New Zealand—Passport required. No visa required for stay up to 90 days.

Niue—Passport, onward/return ticket, and hotel reservation required. Contact New Zealand Embassy for more information.

Norfolk Island—Passport and visa required. Contact Australian Embassy.

Palau—Proof of U.S. citizenship and onward/return ticket required.

Papua New Guinea—Passport and visa required. Visas up to 3 months issued on arrival.

Solomon Islands—Passport onward/return ticket, and proof of sufficient funds required. Two month visitor permit issued on arrival.

Tahiti—See French Polynesia.

Tonga—Passport and onward/return ticket required. No visa required for stay up to 30 days.

Tuvalu—Passport, visa, and onward/return ticket required. Contact British Embassy or Consulate for visa.

Vanuatu—Passport and onward/return ticket required. No visa required for stay up to 30 days. Contact British Embassy or Consulate for information.

Western Samoa—Passport and onward/return ticket required. No visa required for stay up to 30 days.

Chapter 4

Arriving & Departing Foreign Countries

Arrivals

When you arrive in a foreign country you must clear customs and immigration of the country just as you do when returning to the U.S. In some countries, an immigration or customs official will merely wave you through. In other countries, you may undergo a more thorough entry process that can include an examination of your travel documents, baggage, clothes, or person. Countries conduct border examinations for several reasons:

» To determine if you are eligible to enter.
» To make sure that you are not bringing any contraband into the country.
» To see what you are bringing into the country and if you owe any duty on those items.
» To make sure you have enough money to pay for your stay or to make you exchange some of your U.S. currency for the local money.
» To ensure that you will leave.

Immigration

Clearing immigration is a matter of proving who you are, what your nationality is, and that you have permission to enter the country. This is accomplished simply by displaying your passport and a valid visa stamp or tourist card in those countries requiring visas or tourist cards for entry. You may be asked questions about the purpose of your visit, how long you will stay, what areas of the country you will visit, and at what hotel you will be lodging.

Customs

Many countries will require that you make a customs declaration stating what articles you are bringing into the country. Declare items you are carrying even if you are not sure that you are required to do so. Ask questions of the border officials if you do not understand the requirements. If you are asked to make a customs declaration, it is better to play it safe. Many countries have stiff fines or jail penalties for smuggling. Smuggling merely means bringing items into or taking items out of a country illegally or without paying the required import or export duty.

Caution. Never carry another person's luggage when entering another country. Especially refuse to carry the bags of a person you do not know or just met. Customs officials worldwide will consider bags and their contents to be the property of the person carrying them into the country. You will be held responsible for any violations found inside of bags belonging to another person that you carry. If you do carry someone else's bags, be sure you know the person and that you know and can explain everything that is inside the bag.

If a country uses an entry form on your arrival and gives you a copy, the same form will probably be used as an exit form. Safeguard the form and have it available when you depart the country. You could experience some problems exiting the country without the form.

All countries permit you to bring in duty-free, personal items that you will use during your visit. The standard used by customs services throughout the world is that you may enter a country with items that are "reasonable and appropriate" for your visit. What is reasonable and appropriate depends on the length and purpose of your visit. A foreign customs official may consider your four suitcases reasonable for a two month visit, but unreasonable for a two day visit.

Customs regulations vary country by country, but there are certain items that generally must be declared in any country you enter. Always declare these items.

» Guns
» Prescription drugs
» Currency
» Valuable items like watches, perfume, jewelry, and cameras

Another basic customs principle worldwide is that you can bring into a country duty-free those things that you are going to take out with you. Most countries also allow you a personal exemption to import duty-free small quantities of cigarettes, alcohol, and perfume, and a limited allowance for gifts. You may be charged an import duty in some countries on items that the customs service thinks are beyond your personal needs during your visit or on items that they suspect you will not take out with you when you leave. You may also be charged an import duty on things that you bring in as gifts for someone else or on items to be sold in the country.

If you are charged duty on items you plan to take out when you leave, you may be able to get a refund. To obtain a refund, you will need to prove that you brought the item in, paid duty on it, and are taking it out. Keep any entry forms and duty receipts, and ask the customs official about refund procedures when you are charged duty on an item that you will be taking out. If you are charged duty, most countries will require you to pay the duty in the local currency, a good reason to carry some local currency when you arrive in a foreign country.

Many countries prohibit the importation of certain items. Check import requirements with the foreign embassy of the country you will visit before attempting to enter a country with the following items.

» Pornography

» Alcohol. Many countries, particularly Moslem nations, do not allow alcohol to be imported.

» Firearms, ammunition, explosives, or fireworks

» Items that can carry animal or plant diseases. To prevent the spread of agricultural diseases, most countries are very restrictive on the food products, animals, and plants that you can import.

» Pets. Some countries will not allow you to bring your pet with you at all, but most will, provided that you can prove that your pet has been properly inoculated. You will usually need a veterinary health certificate showing the inoculations. You often need prior approval from the country's agriculture ministry before your pet is admitted. If you arrive without the proper documentation or permission, your pet will usually be quarantined and inoculated. The quarantine will last a month or more for which you will be charged. Even if you have the proper documentation, your pet could still be quarantined. For example, the United Kingdom quarantines all arriving cats and dogs for six months. If you plan to bring your pet overseas, be sure to check with the country's embassy or consulate on their pet entry requirements before traveling. You may find yourself paying for a long quarantine period if you arrive with an animal without the proper clearances.

Currency
Countries with a strong currency black market usually will require that you make a currency declaration on arrival. You will be asked to declare all money, jewelry, cameras, or other valuables. The declaration will then be checked when you depart to ensure that you did not exchange money on the black market or sell your valuables. Be sure to keep all currency transaction receipts for your departure.

Return Ticket/Onward Ticket
Many countries require as a condition of entry that you prove that you will leave. In these countries, proof that you hold an airline ticket to return to the U.S., or an airline, train, or bus ticket to travel forward to another country will be requested of you at the port of entry. The purpose of this requirement is to prevent you from becoming stranded in the country without sufficient funds to get out. Countries do not want you to stay forever or to pay for your transportation to get you to leave. If your plans are such that you do

not have a return/onward ticket, you could be asked to deposit a sum with the immigration officials sufficient to buy a return ticket to the U.S. or an onward ticket to another country.

Departures

Customs And Immigration

Many countries require that you go through customs and immigration when you depart. It is usually not a problem exiting countries as long as you have not overstayed your visa, are not exporting a large quantity of merchandise, or are not trying to remove artifacts, antiques, or artworks of the country. Most countries want you to spend and leave behind as much of your U.S. currency as possible, so there are usually few restrictions on the amount of merchandise you can take out. However, most countries do place limits on the amount of tobacco or alcohol that you can export duty-free.

Be careful if you want to export items that the country considers to have archaeological, historical, artistic, scientific, cultural, or environmental significance. You may need an export permit before you can legally remove these things from a country. Items such as antiques, works of art, furs, and precious metals or stones may require a permit. If you plan to purchase any such items, it is best to first locate the proper ministry within the country and inquire about export restrictions before purchasing. The seller of the item should be able to direct you to the proper government office. You can also check with the U.S. Consulate. They will likely know those items that have export restrictions. Unless you know that the seller is trustworthy, do not simply rely on his or her assurances that the item can be exported. They are interested in making the sale, not in whether you can leave the country with the item. Some unscrupulous dealers have been known to sell tourists an item that they knew could not be exported, then notified customs authorities that the tourist had the item. The item was then confiscated when the tourist tried to depart and sold again and again to other tourists. If you purchase an item that has export restrictions and you do not have a permit to export it, the item may be confiscated by the foreign country when you exit, or by U.S. Customs when you return to the United States (see Chapter 16).

And once again remember to never carry anyone else's bags through any customs checkpoint whether arriving or departing.

Departure Taxes
Many countries will charge you a departure tax when you leave. It may be called an airport tax. In some countries the tax is included in the price of the airline ticket. In other countries you will have to pay at your exit point. Some countries will allow you to pay the tax with hard currency (U.S. dollars); others will only accept local currency. Save some local currency to pay the departure tax unless you know U.S. money will be accepted. After paying the departure tax, you can convert your remaining local currency back to U.S. dollars. In fact, some countries will require that you do so, as they prohibit the export of their currency.

Chapter 5

Help From American Consuls Abroad

Many countries establish foreign service posts in other countries. The foreign service post in a country's capital city is the embassy. Consulates general and consulates are regional offices of embassies. Consulates general are posts located in large cities other than the capital city; consulates are posts in smaller cities. Each embassy and most consulates general and consulates have a consular section. Thus the term "consulate" can mean the consular section in an embassy, consulate general, or consulate.

A consul or consular officer is an official representative of a government residing in a foreign country. Consular officers have two primary functions:

» They issue visas to foreigners.
» They help their own citizens abroad.

The United States has assigned consular officers to foreign posts around the world. They are employees of the Department of State (or State Department). There are 164 U.S. Embassies in capital cities of the world. There are also 67 U.S. Consulates General and 19 U.S. Consulates around the world.

U.S. consuls are U.S. citizens. They serve a tour of duty in the foreign country normally lasting two to four years. U.S. consuls are often assisted by local employees who are citizens of the host country but employed by the United States. Because of the large workload and small number of consuls, you may be assisted by a non-U.S. citizen if you seek help from a U.S. consular section.

When To Register With A U.S. Embassy Or Consulate

Registration at the consular section in the countries you visit makes your presence and whereabouts in the country known to U.S. officials. This will make it easier for a consular employee to contact you in an emergency. During a disaster or unrest overseas, U.S. consular officers will assist in locating and evacuating Americans, if they know Americans are in the country. Registration also makes it easier to replace a lost or stolen passport.

The State Department recommends that U.S. citizens register with the consular section of the nearest embassy, consulate general, or consulate in the following circumstances:

» When you plan to stay in a country for longer than one month.

» If you find yourself in a country or area that is experiencing civil unrest, has an unstable political climate, or has experienced a natural disaster like an earthquake or hurricane.

» If you plan to visit a country where there are no U.S. foreign posts. In this case you should register at the U.S. consular section in an adjacent country, leave an itinerary of your travels, and inquire about the conditions in the country you plan to visit. Consular officials can tell you if any third country consulate will be able to assist you in the country you will visit.

If you are traveling with an escorted tour to areas experiencing political unrest or other problems, find out if your tour operator registered with the American Consulate for you. If not, or if you are traveling on your own, leave a copy of your itinerary with the nearest consular section soon after your arrival.

What U.S. Consuls Do For Americans Traveling Abroad

U.S. consuls provide a variety of services to Americans who experience difficulties while traveling abroad. Contact a U.S. consulate section for these services.

Replace Your Passport
A U.S. consul can replace a lost or stolen passport, usually within 24 hours. If you think your passport was stolen, you should first report the theft to the local police and obtain a police declaration of the theft to take with you to the U.S. Consulate. If you lose your passport abroad, the more identification and proof of citizenship you can provide to the consular officer, the easier it will be to obtain a replacement passport. See Chapter 1, *Passports*, for details on replacing lost passports.

Help You Find Medical Assistance
If you get sick, are injured, or need other medical care while overseas, a consular officer can provide a list of local doctors, dentists, medical specialists, clinics, or hospitals. If you are seriously ill or injured, a consul will help you find medical assistance, and if you request, inform your family or friends in the U.S. about your condition. In an emergency when you are unable to communicate, the consul will check your passport for the name and address of the person in the U.S. you designated to be contacted in an emergency, and contact that person about your condition.

Help You Get Money If You Become Destitute
If you lose (or spend) all your money while abroad, consular officers can help you contact your family, bank, or employer to arrange for them to send you funds. In some cases these funds can be wired to you through the State Department.

Get A Message To You About An Emergency At Home
Your family, friends, or employer may need to reach you because of an emergency at home or because they are worried about your welfare. They should call the State Department's Citizens

Emergency Center at (202) 647-5225. The State Department will relay the message to the consular officer in the country in which you are traveling. A consular officer will attempt to locate you, pass on the urgent message, and report back to your family, friends, or employer if doing so does not violate your privacy.

Visit You In Jail

If you are ever arrested in a foreign country, you should ask the authorities to notify a U.S. consul. When you are in a foreign country you are subject to the laws of that country and consuls cannot get you out of jail. They can work to protect your interests and rights. Consuls can provide you a list of local attorneys, visit you in jail, explain local laws in general terms, and contact your family, friends, or employer. A consular officer can arrange to transfer money, food, and clothing to the prison authorities from your family and friends. They will also try to protect you from inhumane or unhealthy conditions.

Help You In A Disaster Or Evacuation

Consuls will assist Americans in dealing with natural disasters or civil unrest abroad. If you are safe after such an event has occurred but are unable to contact your relatives, you should contact the U.S. Consulate to inform them of your condition. Your relatives back home will be worried. The U.S. consul will pass a message about your condition to your family through the State Department. Commercial transportation entering or leaving a country can be disrupted during times of unrest or disaster. If this happens and the State Department thinks it is unsafe for Americans to remain in the country, consuls will set up evacuation transportation for Americans. The U.S. Government cannot order Americans to leave a foreign country. The State Department will only advise that they believe a country is unsafe and try to assist those who choose to leave.

Death Abroad

When an American dies abroad, a consular officer will notify the deceased's family and inform them about options and costs for local burial or return of the body to the United States. Costs for returning a body to the U.S. are high and must be paid by the family. Often local laws and procedures make returning a body to the U.S. for burial a lengthy process. The U.S. Government will not pay for local burial or shipment of remains to the United States.

Non-Emergency Services
Consular officers provide U.S. citizens a variety of non-emergency services. These include providing travel warnings, assisting with absentee voting and Selective Service registration, notarizing documents, advising on property claims, and providing U.S. tax forms. You may also be able to get advice and answers concerning specific conditions or local practices of the country you are visiting.

If you need consular help but are not near a U.S. Consulate, try contacting the consulate of another nation that is on friendly terms with the U.S., such as a British, Canadian, or Australian Consulate. They may be willing to contact the U.S. Consulate and help arrange the assistance you need.

You need to help consuls assist you should you need their help. Before you begin your trip, complete the address page in the front of your passport. Provide the name, address and telephone number of someone to be contacted in an emergency. Do it in pencil so that you can change the person to be contacted if necessary. Do not give the names of anyone traveling with you in case the entire party experiences the same difficulties or are all involved in an accident.

What U.S. Consuls Will Not Do For Americans Traveling Abroad

Consular officers give priority to Americans in the most serious legal, medical, or financial difficulties. They are not there to provide all the types of assistance that you may need while traveling abroad. Do not rely on U.S. consuls to provide routine or commercially available services. U.S. consular officers do not issue visas to U.S. citizens to travel to other countries. You have to get those visas from the consular office of the country you will visit. Consular officers will not act as travel agents, tourist information bureaus, banks, lawyers, investigators, or law enforcement officers. They will not make travel or hotel reservations, cash personal or traveler's checks, or lend you money. Consular officers cannot supply you with medications or pay for your medical or hospital expenses. They will not help you find employment or get a visa, residence permit, or driving permit. Consular officers will not act as interpreters, search for missing luggage, call your credit card company or bank, replace stolen travelers checks, or settle disputes with local merchants. You cannot use a U.S. consul to pick up mail or messages while traveling. However, consular officers will tell you how to get help on these and other matters.

The Citizens Emergency Center

The State Department's Bureau of Consular Affairs operates the Citizens Emergency Center in Washington, D.C. The Center deals with emergencies involving Americans abroad—Americans who die, become destitute, get sick, disappear, have accidents, or get arrested.

The Citizens Emergency Center is the point of contact in the U.S. for family members and others who are concerned about an American's condition abroad. The Center receives many inquiries from worried relatives who have not heard from a traveler or who need to contact a traveler about a family crisis at home. This is also the State Department's focal point for major disasters such as plane crashes, terrorist incidents, and natural disasters that have involved Americans abroad. The Center receives and passes information concerning Americans abroad through U.S. Embassies and Consulates.

You can reach the Citizens Emergency Center by telephone at (202) 647-5225. The Center is open 8:15 a.m. to 10:00 p.m., Monday through Friday; and 9:00 a.m. to 3:00 p.m. on Saturday (Eastern time). At other times, including Federal holidays, you can reach a State Department duty officer at (202) 634-3600. Before traveling overseas, consider giving these numbers to relatives or friends in case it becomes necessary for them to locate you or check on your welfare during your trip.

Chapter 6

Money Matters

Foreign Currency

Most countries restrict the amount of their own currency that travelers or residents are allowed to import or export. Generally, Western nations allow larger amounts of their own currency to be carried in or out while less developed nations have tighter restrictions on currency import and export. A few do not allow you to enter with any of their currency. Currency restrictions can change. To find out about the most current currency restrictions, check with a large bank, foreign exchange firm, travel agent, or the embassy or consulate of the countries you plan to visit.

Most countries will welcome your U.S. dollars and may require that you convert some dollars to the local currency upon arrival. U.S. and Canadian dollars, Japanese yen, and some Western European currencies are the "hard currencies;" money that is universally in demand and trusted. The "soft currencies" are all the others. Countries would like you to bring in and leave within their borders as much hard currency as possible. They also want you to exchange your hard currency at the official exchange rate, not on the black market (if a currency black market exists).

The difference in the official and black market exchange rates can be significant, as much as ten times. Deciding whether to exchange money on the black market is a personal choice, but be aware of potential problems of such exchanges. You could be cheated by currency street vendors and you would have no recourse since the exchange you tried to make was illegal in the first place. The street vendor may be cooperating with the authorities in a sting operation to catch foreigners violating the country's currency laws. Counterfeiters also know that most travelers are not familiar with the look and feel of the local currency. You could be given counterfeit money if you exchange currency on the black market.

Those countries that have currency black markets often require that you declare all the money you are carrying when you enter and again when you exit. The purpose is to see how much hard currency you brought in and exchanged and to ensure that you exchanged money at the official exchange rates. You may be asked to show receipts of your currency exchanges when you leave. Keep all exchange receipts until you have exited. You may also need these receipts to exchange the local currency back into hard currency at your departure. Some countries with tight currency controls will not permit you to convert the local currency back into dollars when you leave. They also may not permit you to export their currency, so you will have to spend it or leave it behind.

To avoid the problems associated with exchanging foreign currency and to get the most value for your money, it is usually best to:

» Only exchange your currency for the local currency in amounts that you think you will need or the minimum you are required to exchange upon entering. Remember, it always costs money to exchange money.

» Consider charging most expenses to your credit card where possible. When you pay by credit card, you eliminate the need to exchange large sums of money and save yourself the currency exchange costs.

» Plan your expenditures so that you arrive at your departure point with just a small amount of local currency. However, be sure to save some local currency for departure expenses like taxis, tips, and departure taxes.

» Try to use coins before using paper notes towards the end of your trip, or use coins for tips, gifts, or souvenirs. Coins usually are not accepted at currency exchanges.

» Avoid currency violations. Currency violations are normally dealt with in two ways. Violators may be fined **plus** the money involved in the currency violation may be confiscated. Arrest, especially if large sums are involved, is also a possibility. Not a good way to end your trip.

Bringing Money Abroad

Traveler's Checks

To avoid carrying a large amount of cash overseas, take most of your money in the form of traveler's checks. If possible, obtain traveler's checks in the currencies of the countries you plan to visit. Traveler's checks in U.S. currency are normally accepted overseas, but often only at banks, hotels, or currency exchange houses. You can usually find traveler's checks in the U.S. for these foreign currencies: Canadian dollars, English pounds, French francs, German marks, Japanese yen, and Swiss francs. Because it is a very stable currency, foreign exchange experts recommend carrying Swiss franc traveler's checks if you are traveling to countries other than those listed above.

Large banks in most cities will have a foreign exchange counter that deals in foreign traveler's checks. You can also get foreign denomination traveler's checks at American Express offices, some AAA offices, and through currency exchange companies. Ruesch International, a currency exchange firm, will provide foreign traveler's checks by mail. Call (800) 424-2923 for information about this service.

With traveler's checks in the currency of the countries you are visiting, you can readily cash checks with merchants without paying a service fee and without worrying about the exchange rate you are getting. Most foreign banks will charge a fee to cash traveler's checks, whether made out in U.S. or the country's currency. Your hotel will probably be willing to convert your U.S. currency traveler's check to the local currency, but usually at an unfavorable (to you) exchange rate. If you plan to visit several European countries, try to plan your expenses and get some traveler's checks in the currencies of the different countries you will visit.

Cash
Before you depart, try to purchase a small amount of foreign currency so that you have the local cash immediately available for taxi fares, tips, and phone calls. After a long international flight, you will want to avoid standing in line at the currency exchange counter of a foreign airport. However, buy foreign currency in the U.S. only if the country you are visiting allows travelers to bring in the country's currency. Get some currency at your bank when you buy traveler's checks, at a foreign exchange firm, or at foreign exchange windows in U.S. airports. A bank is your best choice if they have the currency you need since they charge less than foreign exchange firms.

Large banks will usually carry about 25 of the world's major currencies. At a bank you should be able to get currency for most Western European nations, Australia, New Zealand, Canada, Mexico, Costa Rica, Hong Kong, Japan, Korea, Singapore, Taiwan, and Thailand. If you need other foreign currencies, your bank may be able to special order them for you. Foreign exchange firms carry or can get currencies for over 120 countries.

When you buy foreign currency in the U.S., ask for a variety of denominations, especially small bills. You want to have small bills when you arrive for expenses like tips and taxi fares. You can help prevent being taken advantage of by studying the money before you leave. You should be able to recognize the bills and have a general idea of how much each is worth in U.S. dollars.

If you are unable to get foreign denomination bills, carry some small denomination U.S. bills for your immediate arrival expenses. U.S. money will usually be accepted (even welcomed) as payment for taxis and tips. One word of caution; it is illegal in some countries to use any currency other than the country's own.

Important. If you leave the U.S. with more than $10,000 in any form—cash, checks in bearer form, money orders, or traveler's checks—you must file a report with U.S. Customs at the time of departure. A check in bearer form is a negotiable check made out to cash or endorsed by the payee. You can take any sum of money out of the country, but you must report large sums. Use Customs Form 4790, available at ports of entry, to file the report. If you do not report money in excess of $10,000 taken out of the country, Customs can seize your money and bring civil or criminal actions against you. Many travelers are surprised to undergo an inspection by U.S. Customs while waiting for their plane to depart the U.S. It can and does happen. Customs is attempting to disrupt the flow of money out of the country earned in the international drug trade or from other illegal activities. The same reporting requirements apply if you bring more than $10,000 into the U.S. See Chapter 17.

Personal Checks

Generally, personal checks will not be accepted abroad and travelers should not count on using this method to meet their money needs. There are exceptions for travelers who are affiliated with an organization or institution that has offices abroad. For instance, American Express card holders can cash personal checks at overseas American Express offices.

Credit Cards

Major U.S. credit cards can be used for purchases or cash advances worldwide, but only in certain locations. Credit cards are still not readily accepted in many parts of the world outside of tourist and business centers, despite the claims of the credit card company commercials. Do not assume your credit card will be accepted. This problem arises most often at small hotels at checkout when the traveler is surprised to learn that his or her credit card will not be accepted. Be sure your particular credit card will be accepted before relying on this method to pay your expenses.

When you charge a purchase overseas, the way the charge is converted to U.S. dollars depends on the credit card issuer. Most credit cards will convert the foreign amount to dollars at the exchange rate on the day the bill is processed by the foreign bank. Some cards will convert the foreign amount to dollars on the day the bill is processed at the credit card company. Whichever method is used, the bill is often not processed on the day of the purchase so the rate of exchange on your bill may be different from the rate when you made the purchase. If the dollar has fallen or risen against the currency for which you made the charge purchase, you will be billed more or less than you expected.

Keep track of your credit card purchases so you do not exceed your limit. Some countries consider it to be fraud when a purchaser attempts to make a purchase over their available credit limit. The State Department reports that Americans have been arrested in some countries for exceeding their credit limit.

If you are traveling for more than one month, your credit card bill will arrive at your home or post office while you are away. If you do not make some arrangements, the bill will be waiting for you unpaid and overdue while you may be trying to use the card in a foreign country. You could find your credit privileges suspended when you need the card the most and you will find it difficult to correct the problem from abroad. Do one of two things to avoid this problem. You can make an advance payment to cover your charges while traveling. Be sure that your credit card company knows what you are doing before sending an advance payment. The other option is to have the bill sent to your work, a friend, or family member and arrange for them to make a payment for you.

ATMs

Using automatic teller machines for cash needs abroad is quickly becoming the best way to convert dollars to foreign currency. It is a good way to get foreign currency because the exchange rate is usually the wholesale rate that is offered to banks but usually not available to individuals. Major automatic teller machine systems and American Express are continually increasing their networks of international ATMs. Before leaving, check with your bank or ATM network on the availability and location of ATM machines in the countries you will be visiting.

ATMs abroad work like ATMs in the U.S. You need to find a machine linked to your bank's network. Most foreign ATMs will have instructions in English to guide you through the transaction. The machines dispense bills in the local currency and will immediately debit your account in the U.S. ATMs outside of North America normally do not accept a PIN number longer than 4 digits. If your PIN is longer than 4 digits, arrange with your bank for a new number before you leave. Also, most foreign ATM keyboards have numbers only, not letters. If you use letters for your PIN, convert to numbers using the same number/letter scheme on your phone pad.

Foreign ATMs often automatically debit your main checking account without giving you the opportunity to choose to make the withdrawal from another account. Be sure you have funds available in your checking account to cover withdrawals.

Virtually every bank will charge a transaction fee for an overseas withdrawal. The fee will be about $2 per transaction regardless of the amount withdrawn. You will save on transaction fees by making a few large transactions rather than several small ones. However, be cautious in carrying large amounts of cash. It may be safer to make more ATM withdrawals and pay the transaction fees.

Transferring Money Abroad From The U.S.

American Express and Western Union will wire funds from the U.S. to many, but not all countries. This is an almost instantaneous transfer of money. It is especially useful when you need to send or receive cash immediately while abroad. The transfer can be accomplished by telephone and charged to a credit card. Payment is made to the recipient in the currency of the country where the money is sent. The money is wired and available for pick up at an American Express or Western Union office, an affiliated office, or at a foreign bank or post office. To transfer money, contact any American Express or Western Union office with the specific destination of where the money is to be sent.

Another way to transfer money is to make a wire transfer from your bank through an overseas bank. This method will probably take a bit longer, usually at least one day to complete the transaction. Carry the telephone number of your local bank and your account number to accomplish a bank wire transfer.

Value Added Tax (VAT)

You will encounter the Value Added Tax in Europe, Japan, and many other countries. In Canada it is called Goods and Services Tax (GST). It could go by different names in other countries. VAT is a tax imposed on every step of producing a product. It can add considerably, up to 33%, to the total price you pay for items purchased abroad. Travelers can often obtain a refund of some or all of the VAT that they pay. Generally, you are eligible for a refund if you take the items that you purchased out of the country when you leave. Usually your purchases must exceed a minimum amount established by each country. In some countries the minimum applies to your entire visit. In other countries you must make minimum purchases per store, or even per item, to qualify for a VAT refund. Travelers can usually obtain VAT refunds for merchandise purchases only, not for food, lodging, or transportation. In Canada, you can get a GST refund for lodging in some provinces.

The VAT rate varies country to country, ranging from 6% to 33%. Procedures for obtaining a VAT refund also vary. You can inquire about the specific refund procedures while you are in the country. To find out before you arrive, contact the embassy, consulate, or tourist office. Once you are out of the country, you normally can no longer apply for the refund. Canada is one exception. See below.

Obtaining A VAT Refund
Generally, there are four ways to obtain a VAT refund.

Europe Tax-Free Shopping (ETS). If you are traveling in one of 15 participating European countries, the easiest way to get a VAT refund is through the European tax refund service called ETS. Look for a blue and red "Tax Free For Tourists" sign in English in store windows. Participating merchants will issue a VAT refund check at the time of your purchase. You can then cash refund checks at ETS counters at major transportation terminals. Try to cash checks made out in a foreign currency before you leave the country. You may have trouble cashing small foreign currency checks at U.S. banks. Also the bank service charge for processing the check and the poor exchange rate you will get may eat up most of the refund.

By Mail. When you purchase an item that includes VAT, show your passport to the seller and ask for a VAT refund form. Fill it out and get a copy. You may have to furnish your own VAT refund forms available from the country's customs service or tourist office. When you depart, a customs officer must check your purchases and validate on your form that you are leaving with the items. You then mail the validated form back to the seller who mails you a refund check or credits your charge card. If a country uses this method, try to pay for your purchases with a credit card. That way your refund is credited to your account in U.S. currency and you will not have to pay a bank a service charge to convert a foreign denomination check.

Refund on Departure. This is similar to the mail refund method except that you get your refund in cash before leaving the country after the country's customs service validates your purchases. This method is usually available only at major airports or seaports.

Deduct VAT at Time of Purchase. Some countries allow you to deduct the VAT from the price you pay immediately if the merchant mails the merchandise directly to you. International shipping is expensive so this method only makes sense if you were planning to ship the item home, rather than hand carry it back with you.

You will have to decide whether it is worth the time and effort to pursue VAT refunds. It probably is if you make significant merchandise purchases, but can be a lot of trouble for small amounts. You will need to allow extra time when you make purchases and at the border to process your VAT refund. Canada is an exception as GST refunds are relatively easy. Just save your receipts showing GST paid, obtain and complete a simple GST refund form and mail it to Revenue Canada after you return to the U.S. You will receive a GST refund *paid in U.S. funds*. In Newfoundland, Nova Scotia, and Ontario, you must also complete separate provincial application forms to obtain a refund of the provincial tax.

Chapter 7

Driving Abroad

Driving conditions throughout the world vary considerably. In some countries driving conditions will be comparable to driving in the U.S. In others, roads are not built to U.S. standards, are more crowded with cars, trucks, bicycles, and pedestrians, and traffic laws are frequently less strict or less well enforced. Exercise care when driving, especially in less developed countries. Traffic accidents are the leading cause of death or injury for U.S. overseas travelers. See Chapter 14 for additional information.

Many travelers who drive overseas are surprised (or shocked) at the price of gasoline. In most countries, gasoline is much more expensive than in the U.S., often at least twice as expensive. If you plan to drive, be sure that you have budgeted enough money for gasoline expenses.

In some countries you will encounter a road tax. It is charged to all drivers upon entering the country at the customs checkpoint. After you pay the tax you receive a sticker or placard that must be displayed whenever you drive within the country.

Members of the American Automobile Association (AAA) can obtain many AAA-type services in 110 countries through foreign auto clubs affiliated with AAA. Some of the foreign auto clubs provide

AAA members the full range of services offered to members in the United States: emergency road service, maps and travel publications, and general touring information. In other countries the services offered are much more limited. Some foreign auto clubs charge a fee for some services. Contact an AAA office for a list of covered countries and the services offered in each country. Ask for the free booklet entitled, *Offices To Serve You Abroad*.

Insurance

Unless you are driving in Canada, your automobile insurance policy will almost certainly **not** cover you while driving abroad. U.S. insurance policies generally do not cover driving in Mexico. If you drive abroad without making insurance arrangements, you will be driving uninsured. You can obtain a supplemental policy either through an insurance company—your own or one specializing in international auto insurance—or through a car rental company. If you obtain a policy through a car rental company, be sure that it provides liability coverage for you. Some car rental insurance may only cover damage to the car, not property damage or personal injuries that you may cause with the vehicle.

If you plan to drive through more than one country and you obtain insurance through a car rental company, be sure that the insurance covers you if you drive out of the country. Policies offered by car rental companies may only cover you in the country in which you rented the car. Also be sure that any insurance policy covers all individuals in your party who may drive during your travels. You do not want to have insurance coverage only to find after an accident that the person driving was not covered by the policy.

Check with your credit card company to see if they cover collision damage to rental cars when the car rental fees are charged to the card. If they do, you can avoid taking the collision damage waiver, or CDW, coverage from the rental company. CDW charges can be $7-$15 per day. CDW only provides coverage for damage to the rental car. Many credit card companies have recently dropped the collision damage coverage that they previously offered. Check with your credit card issuer before assuming that you are automatically covered when you rent a car with a credit card.

Driver's Licenses

You will be able to drive overseas in many countries with only your state driver's license. Some countries also require that you hold an International Driving Permit before driving. Even if it is not required, you may still find it helpful to obtain an International Driving Permit before leaving the U.S. This document contains some of the information on your driver's license translated into nine different languages. Carrying an International Driving Permit may make it easier to rent a car or deal with the police if you are stopped for traffic infractions abroad. Contact the embassies or tourist offices of the countries you will be driving in to determine if you need an International Driving Permit. You have to get the permit while you are in the U.S. If a country does not permit you to drive on a state driver's license and you need to drive, you will have to get a license issued by that country—potentially a big hassle that you want to avoid.

An International Driving Permit is cheap and easy to obtain. It may be required, and if not, it may help ease your travels. So if you plan to drive overseas, it is a good idea to get one. The easiest way to get a permit is through an American Automobile Association (AAA) office. You do not have to be a member to get a permit through AAA. You do need to apply in person and bring a valid U.S. driver's license and two passport photos. Most AAA offices can take passport photos for you. The fee for an International Driving Permit is about $10. Some visa service companies will also issue the permits.

Maps

Many international travelers carry maps of their destinations. When you drive abroad, good road maps become a necessity. You may be able to get road maps of your destination from the country's tourist office. See Appendix D for locations. Travelers who are AAA members can pick up road maps for the more commonly visited countries from their local AAA office. For maps of both common and uncommon destinations, try Map Link, a mail order map supplier that carries maps for virtually every area of the world. Contact Map Link at 25 East Mason Street, Santa Barbara, California 93101, (805) 965-4402. Many travel bookstores also have or can get international road maps.

Chapter 8

Keeping In Touch

Some people want to get away from it all when they travel. Others want or need to keep in touch with friends, family, or work while abroad. This chapter describes how to keep in touch with people in the U.S. while traveling overseas.

Sending Mail

Inquire locally at your hotel or find a post office to be sure you have the correct postage on any letters or packages you mail from abroad to the U.S. You need postage for international mail, not domestic. Unless you are very patient, always send international mail by air mail. Be sure "par avion" is written or imprinted on any letters you send. Par avion is the internationally recognized French term for air mail. Even by air mail, letters and packages can take a long time to reach the U.S. from many countries.

Place postage on correspondence yourself to ensure that air mail, not regular mail postage is used. Some travelers have found that the cheaper postage was used when they have paid for, but did not personally affix air mail stamps. Presumably the person doing the affixing pocketed the difference.

Large U.S. express delivery companies (e.g. Federal Express, UPS) also operate in many foreign countries. Consider using these services, where available, to send urgent or important documents and packages to the United States.

Receiving Mail

There are a several of ways to receive mail while abroad.

Local Resident. If you are staying with a local resident, simply have the mail sent to you in care of that person.

Hotel. You can provide the address of your hotel to your contacts and have mail sent there. The envelope should show your name and be marked "To Be Held For Arrival." When you register and check out, ask if any mail is waiting for you.

Post Office. You can also have mail sent to the main post office in the city you are visiting. Mail sent to you at an overseas post office should be marked "Poste Restante," which is the international term for General Delivery. It should also be marked "To Be Called For." When you go to the post office to pick up mail, you will need to identify yourself with your passport. When people send you mail through an overseas post office, try to have them address the envelope with your name exactly as it appears on your passport. This will help avoid any question that the mail is yours.

American Express. Some American Express offices overseas will accept and hold mail for you. Card holders and traveler's check and travel service customers receive this service free of charge. Others will be charged a fee. Letters sent to American Express offices should be marked "Client Hold." American Express will accept letters and telegrams only. No parcels, registered mail, or recorded deliveries are accepted. To determine which American Express offices offer letter hold service, call or visit an American Express office and ask for the free booklet entitled, *American Express Worldwide Traveler's Companion*. This booklet contains a complete listing of American Express offices worldwide and shows those that have letter hold service.

The State Department says that U.S. Embassies and Consulates do not accept and hold mail for U.S. citizens traveling overseas. You may find that certain embassies or consulates, especially in less visited countries, will hold your mail. If you have no other options to receive mail, it is worth a try, but it is best not to rely on this method.

Whichever method you use to receive mail, ask the sender to address the envelope by printing or typing. Longhand writing styles often differ throughout the world. You will have a better chance of receiving mail that is easily readable.

Telephones

The telephone systems in most of the world will not be of the same quality and standards as phone systems in the U.S. Procedures for making telephone calls vary country by country. If you cannot figure out the phone system or get a local to explain it to you, try to reach an English-speaking operator. Most foreign telephone books will help you here. The phone books of many countries have a section in English that will tell you how to dial an English-speaking operator. Once you have connected with an operator, you should be able to complete your call.

Telephone calls made in foreign countries are usually much more expensive than comparable calls made in the U.S. The best way to keep your telephone expenses down is to not make calls. If possible, have people call you, rather than making outgoing calls.

Hotel Surcharges

Calling from your hotel room overseas and billing the call to your room account can be especially expensive. Many hotels add huge service charges to the cost of the call. These surcharges can be 250% to 300% of the cost of the call. This is in addition to the cost for the call charged by the telephone company, often a small, local company with unattractive rates. Some travelers in Europe have been shocked to be presented with a phone bill that totaled more than the room bill.

To avoid these huge surcharges, some travelers charge the call to their phone card instead of their room in an attempt to route the call through their own phone company. This method does not always work. Some hotels will still direct your phone card calls through a small, independent long distance carrier. You will usually be charged an excessive rate for the call and the hotel will receive a kickback from the phone company. The difference in price for an overseas call carried by AT&T, Sprint, or MCI, and a call routed through a small local carrier can be quite large. For example, an international call costing about $6 on AT&T can cost over $15 if made through your hotel's phone company.

To be sure that a call you make is being carried by the long distance company you want, make the call then listen for your company's unique dial tone or message. If you hear something different or nothing at all, your call is probably being routed through another long distance company at much higher rates. Hang up immediately and insist that your hotel route your call through your preferred carrier or make the call from another location.

Direct Dial Programs
The major U.S. long distance carriers have tried to combat the customer gouging that occurs overseas by instituting direct dial programs. These programs allow you to make calls directly from abroad to the U.S. or directly between two foreign countries. You dial your long distance company toll-free and are connected to an English-speaking long distance company operator in the U.S. (or an English language voice prompt). Each country has a different toll-free access code. The operator will request the number you want to reach and how you want to bill the call. Your call will then be connected and it will be carried by your chosen long distance carrier at their rates.

The direct dial programs are available for calls made from many countries, but not all. AT&T has the most participating countries, more than 120. MCI's program has about 80 countries. From participating countries, you can always make direct dial calls to the U.S. On a more limited basis, you can also make direct dial calls from one country to another through a U.S. operator. The AT&T program can directly connect calls between about 65 countries. To find out which countries participate in your long distance carrier's direct dial program and to obtain direct dial access codes for the countries you will visit, simply call your carrier's toll-free customer service number.

The numbers of the major U.S. long distance companies with direct dial programs are:

» AT&T: 1-800-331-1140
» MCI: 1-800-828-5458
» Sprint: 1-800-877-4646

To reduce your overseas telephone costs try these methods:

» Stay off the phone.
» Call collect, if your hotel permits collect calls.
» Use a credit card or phone card, again if the hotel permits.
» Make calls from a public phone that will make international calls. You may find these in post offices, airports, train stations, or in international telegraph offices. You can use your calling card or pay with cash, and you will not have to pay the local telephone company surcharges on calls made from these facilities.
» Use a dial direct to the U.S. program offered by a major long distance carrier.

Chapter 9

Travel Insurance

Travel insurance provides coverage for losses that travelers may experience while outside of the U.S. Many international travelers do not carry travel insurance. It is something to at least consider. Your need for travel insurance will depend on where you are going, how you are traveling, and your financial resources should you experience a problem.

Probably the most important reason to carry travel insurance is to fill in the gaps of your health insurance policy. If you become ill or injured overseas, hospitalization and medical treatment can be very costly and you may not be covered by your normal health insurance. Many U.S. health insurance policies are not valid outside the U.S. Also, the Social Security Medicare program does not cover hospital and medical services outside the United States. Even if your health insurance does cover you abroad, it will not cover all expenses. For instance, your health insurance almost certainly will not cover the cost to medically evacuate you from overseas to the U.S. An international medical evacuation can easily cost $15,000.

Before you leave, check your health insurance policy to be sure that it covers medical services abroad. If your health insurance policy does not cover you abroad, or if you need any other kinds of insurance coverage including supplemental health coverage, consider purchasing a temporary traveler's insurance policy.

Travel Insurance Types

Travel insurance coverage can be divided into three basic types: medical expense coverage, coverage for other problems that travelers might experience, and travel assistance programs.

Medical expense insurance normally covers:
» Payment of medical and hospital expenses for treatment of an injury or illness occurring while abroad
» Medical evacuation to the U.S.
» Advance payment of medical expenses
» Prescription drugs
» Emergency dental treatment
» Payment of transportation for a family member to travel overseas to assist you after an injury or illness
» In the case of death, the costs of returning the deceased home

Nonmedical traveler's insurance normally covers:
» Trip interruption, delay, or cancellation
» Flight insurance
» Lost baggage
» Legal assistance
» Personal accident coverage for loss of life, limbs, or sight

Traveler's assistance programs. Most travel insurance plans provide traveler's assistance programs. These programs offer travelers a 24-hour worldwide network of English-speaking contacts who will assist members in emergencies. Contact is made through a toll-free telephone number. Traveler's assistance services usually include:

» 24 hour telephone help from English-speaking operators
» Referral to English-speaking doctors, hospitals, and dentists
» Assistance in obtaining emergency cash
» Emergency messages transmitted to your family, physician, or employer
» Travel document replacement
» Legal referral

You can purchase traveler's insurance that covers only medical expenses abroad or you can obtain a comprehensive policy covering many kinds of travel losses. Policies are issued to cover the number of days of your trip. Medical-only policies cost about $2 to $5 per day per person depending on the level of coverage. Typical medical expense coverage levels are $50,000 or $100,000. The comprehensive policies can cost up to $15 per person per day.

Travel Insurance Sources

There are several sources of travel insurance. Some companies offer this insurance as one of many kinds of insurance offered while others specialize in travel insurance. Many credit cards, especially gold cards, provide some degree of travel insurance to card holders. The coverages offered are usually those shown under the travel assistance category above. The credit card companies may also replace lost tickets if purchased with their card.

You can obtain travel insurance from your travel agent or directly from an insurance company. Listed below are some of the companies offering travel insurance. The listing is not an endorsement of any company.

Access America Inc.
600 Third Avenue, Box 807
New York, NY 10163
800-851-2899

American Express
Travel Protection Plan
1650 Los Gamos Drive
San Rafael, CA 94903
800-234-0375

Carefree Travel Insurance
120 Mineola Blvd., Box 310
Mineola, NY 11501
800-645-2424

Global Assistance Network
999 Summer St.
Stamford, CT 06905
800-368-2110

Health Care Abroad
243 Church St. NW
Suite 100D
Vienna, VA 22180
800-237-6615

International SOS Assistance
Box 11568
Philadelphia, PA 19116
800-523-6586 OR 800-523-8930

International Travelers' Assistance
Box 10623
Towson, MD 212204
800-732 5309

Nationwide/Worldwide
Emergency Ambulance Return
1900 N. MacArthur Blvd.
Oklahoma City, OK 71327
800-654-6700

Travel Insurance

Tele-Trip Co.
Mutual of Omaha
3201 Farnham St.
Omaha, NE 68131
800-228-9792

Travel Assistance International
1133 15th St. NW
Washington, DC 20005
800-821-2828

Travel Guard International
P.O. Box 1200
Stevens Point, WI 54481
800-826-1300

Travel Safe Network
201 Mission St., 29th Floor
San Francisco, CA 91405
800-227-3460

The Travelers Insurance Co.
One Tower Square
Hartford CT 06183
800-243-3174

TravMed
Box 10623
Baltimore, MD 21285
800-732-5309

World Care Travel Assistance
1995 W. Commercial Blvd.
Fort Lauderdale, FL 33307
800-521-4882

Chapter 10

Travel Safety Abroad

Most of the millions of Americans traveling abroad each year enjoy trips free of any crime, violence, arrest, or other emergencies. Unfortunately, some Americans are victimized every year, in every country of the world by such acts, just as foreign visitors to the U.S. are sometimes victims of crime while visiting here. Fear of becoming victims of crime or violence abroad prevents some Americans from venturing beyond our borders. It need not be so. With an understanding of the conditions in the areas to be visited and by taking some sensible precautions, travelers can significantly lessen their chances of becoming victimized. Some countries are significantly more dangerous than others. In most countries the risk of being victimized depends to a great extent upon how you travel and which areas you venture into in the countries and cities you visit.

Preparing For A Safe Trip

Country Information
One of the most important travel safety measures you can take is to learn before you go about the current conditions in the countries you will visit. You may learn, for instance, that crime against tourists is particularly high in one area of a country or on one type of public

transportation. You can significantly decrease your chances of becoming victimized simply by avoiding such areas when traveling in that country. Alternatively, if you decide to travel in areas where crime is prevalent, knowledge about the conditions will alert you to the dangers so you can take precautions.

You can obtain information on problems tourists have experienced at your destination from several sources. Travel books and magazine articles on the countries you will visit often discuss crime problems that tourists have encountered. The tourist offices of some countries will provide information on crime problems within their country. Your travel agent can be a good source of current information as many agents keep up on changing conditions in tourist destinations. Travel agents may know of other travelers who have recently returned from your destination and who can share experiences.

Probably the best source of current information is the U.S. State Department. The State Department distributes Consular Information Sheets for every country. Among other topics, the Information Sheets describe the crime and security situation and areas of instability within each country. Travel Warnings are issued when the State Department recommends that Americans avoid travel to a certain country because of crime, violence, terrorism, or other problems. Travel Warnings are only issued for those countries where travel for Americans is considered to be especially dangerous. See Chapter 11 for ways to obtain Consular Information Sheets and Travel Warnings. If you are traveling to an area where conditions are changing rapidly, call the State Department and try to reach a person familiar with the country's situation. Call the Citizens Emergency Center, (202) 647-5225, and ask to be connected with the country's desk officer.

Locate U.S. Embassies And Consulates
Be sure you carry the address and phone number for all U.S. Embassies and Consulates in the countries you will visit. If you are traveling in especially trouble-prone areas, try to locate the nearest embassy or consulate soon after your arrival. The consular section of these offices should be your first point of contact if you experience problems abroad. The primary responsibility of U.S. consuls is to help Americans in serious trouble. See Chapter 5 for a description of what consular offices can do for Americans and Appendix B for addresses and phone numbers of U.S. Embassies and Consulates worldwide.

Packing Precautions

While easier said than done, always try to pack light. Besides being easier on you, traveling light is safer. When you are not burdened with heavy luggage, you can move more quickly away from potential trouble situations. With less luggage, you may have a free hand. You will also become less tired and less likely to set your luggage down where it is an easier target for thieves.

Put your name, address, and phone number both inside and outside each piece of luggage. Use covered luggage tags on the outside to avoid openly displaying your identity or nationality. Some travelers also place a copy of their trip itinerary inside of each bag to help airlines locate them if their bags are misdirected.

To distinguish your luggage, mark it in some distinctive way such as with colored tape or yarn. Besides making it easier to locate your luggage among many similar bags, marking your bags could also discourage a thief at airport luggage counters.

It is also wise to write out an inventory of the contents of your luggage. Keep it in a place separate from your luggage. The inventory will be very useful for making a claim with an airline or your insurance company if your luggage is lost or stolen.

Things To Leave Home
» Expensive or expensive looking jewelry, watches, or other valuables
» Irreplaceable family objects or photographs
» Unnecessary credit cards
» All unnecessary ID or membership cards
» A copy of your itinerary with family or friends in case they need to contact you
» Anything you would hate to lose

Precautions While Traveling Abroad

Protect Your Passport
Your passport is your most important travel document. It identifies you as an American and entitles you to the protection of the U.S. Government while abroad through U.S. Embassies and Consulates.

Do not pack it with your luggage. If your hotel has a safe, leave your passport there while sight-seeing. Carry a photocopy of your passport identification pages instead while you are out in public. Some countries may require that you leave your passport with the hotel staff overnight when you check-in. This is a normal practice and is not cause for concern unless your passport is not returned to you as promised.

Local Laws And Customs
When you leave the United States, you are subject to the laws of the country you are visiting, not U.S. laws. Actions that may be legal or considered minor infractions in the U.S. can be illegal and bring harsh penalties in other countries. That you are a tourist and unaware of local laws may not protect you from prosecution. Be aware of what is considered criminal in the countries you visit. Consult Consular Information Sheets for information on arrests of Americans for any unusual kinds of offenses. Foreign tourist offices will often advise visitors of what is considered illegal within their country.

Drug Violations
Many countries deal harshly with drug offenses and may not distinguish between possession and trafficking. Possession of small amounts of illegal drugs can lead to a long jail sentence. Also be cautious with prescription drugs. You should be safe if you carry prescription drugs abroad that were purchased in the U.S. for your personal use and that are carried in their original labeled container. However, Americans have been arrested for carrying prescription drugs, particularly tranquilizers and amphetamines, that were purchased legally in a country outside of the U.S. and then carried into a second country where the drug was illegal. If possible, bring any necessary prescription drugs from the U.S. in an amount that will last your entire trip. If you use any narcotic or unusual prescription drugs, carrying a letter from your physician describing your condition may prove useful.

Firearms
Virtually all countries restrict the importation of firearms. You will almost certainly need a permit from the embassy or consulate of the country to be visited before you can legally enter with a firearm. Americans most often run into difficulties for illegal firearms

possession in nearby countries—Canada, Mexico, and Caribbean countries. Mexico has especially severe penalties for illegal possession of firearms.

Photography

Many countries restrict photography in certain areas or of certain buildings. You could be detained or your film confiscated for photographing such things as police and military installations, government buildings, border areas, or airport and train stations. If you are unsure, ask an authority before taking photographs.

Safety In Public Places

Subways, train stations, airports, marketplaces, tourist sites, and festivals are places frequented by tourists, and therefore, also frequented by criminals. Be especially aware of the potential for theft of your wallet or bags in crowded places such as these. Less visited or marginal areas of cities can be among the most interesting spots to see, but also may expose you to a greater risk of crime. Traveling in such areas with a group and in daylight will reduce your risk. Avoid short cuts, narrow alleys, or poorly-lit streets. As you move through areas, walk purposefully and confidently. Act as if you know where you are going, even if you are lost. Be wary of strangers who approach you offering bargains, the exchange of money, or to be your guide.

Carry your belongings securely to help prevent theft. Purses tucked under an arm rather than dangling from a strap are more secure. Store valuables in an inside front pocket, money belt, or pouch worn around your waist or shoulder, not in your hip pocket or purse. If you carry your wallet in your pocket, wrapping rubber bands around it will make it more difficult to slip out of your pocket unnoticed. While walking along a street, carry your bag on the inner side of the curb to avoid drive-by purse snatchers. Pickpockets will often have an accomplice. One will attempt to distract you while the other person steals your belongings. Protect your belongings if you are approached and asked questions, bumped, or told that something is wrong with your clothes or belongings. Children or women carrying babies are often pickpockets.

Hotel Safety

There are common sense precautions you can take to protect against theft from your hotel room or deal with a fire emergency. When you check-in ask for a room between the second and seventh floors. Avoiding the ground floor prevents easy access to your room from outside, and fire equipment will usually be able to reach your floor if you avoid floors above the seventh. Keep your hotel room door locked at all times including while you are in the room. If you have visitors that you do not know well, always meet them in the hotel lobby. Do not leave money or valuables in your hotel room when you are out of the room. Use the hotel safe instead. Avoid using the "Maid Service Requested" door knob sign. It advertises that the room is empty. Know where the fire exits are and plan a primary and alternate escape route. Count the doors between your room and the nearest fire exit in case you have to exit through a dark smoke-filled corridor.

Public Transportation Safety

In some countries, tourists using public transportation have been targeted by criminals. Check the Consular Information Sheets for the countries you will visit to see if problems have been reported. It is safest to use taxis with clearly identified official markings or displaying some sort of a license. Try to avoid using as a taxi any vehicle that is not marked as a taxi. Robbery and theft on trains along popular tourist routes has become a major problem in some areas. It is more common at night and on overnight trains. If you occupy a sleeping compartment, lock the door at all times, carry valuables when you leave the compartment, and try to avoid moving about the train at night. When you cannot lock your compartment securely, sleep in shifts with your traveling companion, block the door in some way, or sleep on top of your valuables and tie down your luggage. Do not accept any food or drinks from strangers on busses or trains. Criminals have drugged and then robbed passengers by giving them drug-laced food or drinks.

Driving Safety

To avoid attracting attention when you rent a car, choose a type that is commonly available in the local area. Ask the rental car company if they will remove any markings that identify the vehicle as a rental car. Try to avoid appearing to be a tourist since tourist drivers are often targeted by criminals. Ask the rental car company for advice on avoiding robbery. They should be able to direct you away from especially problem-prone areas.

Unfortunately, carjackings and robberies of motorists are increasing in many areas of the world. You should be suspicious whenever anyone tries to get your attention or flag you down while driving, offers to fix a flat (that they may have caused), or if you are involved in a "fender-bender" accident. These are often ploys to rob you or steal your vehicle. Avoid as much as possible driving at night and never pick up hitchhikers.

If you have the choice, rent a car with power locks and windows. These features give the driver better control over access to the vehicle. An air conditioner is also a safety feature allowing you to drive with the windows closed. Purses have been stolen through open car windows while the car was occupied. Lock the doors at all times too.

Traffic accidents are the leading cause of injury and death of American overseas travelers. Driving conditions are simply more hazardous in many countries than in the U.S. To decrease the risks, consider using other modes of in-country transportation. Trains, offering reliable schedules and relative safety, are the preferred method of transportation of many travelers. If you rent a car, insist on one with seat belts and use them. See Chapters 7 and 14 for additional driving information.

Safekeeping Money And Valuables

Cash is the least safe way to carry your travel funds. Change your traveler's checks or make ATM withdrawals only as you need currency. Displaying large amounts of cash draws attention. Countersign a traveler's check only in the presence of the person who will cash it. If you are unsure that your traveler's check will be accepted, ask first before signing. If you sign it but it is not accepted, the traveler's check is no longer secure as it can be cashed by another person. When you exchange money, deal only with authorized agents. Do not change money on the black market. When you use a credit card, make sure it is returned to you after each transaction and obtain or destroy the carbon copies of the receipt.

Carry as few valuable items as possible. Expensive jewelry, clothes, cameras, and luggage can mark you as a tourist. As much as possible, avoid the appearance of affluence. Be sure that you can conceal inside of your bags any valuables that you do carry. Your valuables are safest when locked in a hotel safe. When you carry money, traveler's checks, or credit cards in public, use a money belt or pouch worn under your clothing.

Terrorism

Terrorist acts are random and unpredictable, making it impossible to completely protect yourself. Unless specifically targeted, victims of terrorism are usually individuals in the wrong place at the wrong time. The chances of being a victim of ordinary crime are actually far higher. Still, travelers can help protect themselves by avoiding being in the wrong places. The best protection is to avoid travel to areas that have a history of terrorist attacks. Heed the warnings issued by the State Department about unsafe travel situations. If you must travel through areas experiencing terrorist actions, try to minimize the time spent in crowded, public areas and avoid obvious terrorist targets such as places where Americans or Westerners are known to congregate.

Chapter 11

State Department Travel Information

The State Department publishes information on the background and conditions of virtually every country of the world. They also issue booklets containing general information of interest to international travelers. This information is free or reasonably priced.

Consular Information Sheets

Consular Information Sheets are usually two to four pages long and provide a general description of individual countries. They give information about a country's physical and cultural characteristics, entry requirements, currency regulations, medical facilities, and prevalence of crime against foreigners. Consular Information Sheets are issued for every country in the world. They are updated periodically, but some may be a year or two old. The sheets are updated more often for those countries in which Americans have experienced travel difficulties or when country conditions have changed rapidly. It is wise for all international travelers to consult Consular Information Sheets before departing, especially for those traveling to unsettled parts of the world.

Travel Warnings

These are warnings issued for U.S. travelers about specific country conditions originating from U.S. Embassy officials in that country. They might describe health or disease problems, political uprisings or unrest, civil wars, frequent crimes committed against foreigners, dangerous weather, natural disasters, or other conditions of interest to U.S. travelers. They are issued irregularly and only for countries or regions of countries for which travel may be difficult or unsafe. Travel Warnings were formerly called Travel Advisories.

There are several methods to obtain Consular Information Sheets or Travel Warnings:

» Call the Citizens Emergency Center 24 hours a day at (202) 647-5225 from a touch-tone phone.

» Send a self-addressed, stamped envelope stating the country or countries for which you want information to: Overseas Citizens Services, Room 4811, Department of State, Washington, D.C. 20520-4818.

» Go to one of the 13 Passport Agencies. They should be posted or available for review.

» If you have a computer with a modem you can dial into the Consular Affairs Bulletin Board where all the Consular Information Sheets and Travel Warnings are posted. The number is (202) 647-9225. Set your communications software to 8-N-1.

» If you have a fax machine, the Bureau of Consular Affairs operates an automated fax information system through which you can receive by fax any of the travel information put out by the State Department. The telephone number is (202) 647-3000. When you dial the automated fax service you will be given a series of prompts to select the information you wish to receive. There is no charge for the service except for the cost of a long distance phone call. For further information or for a printed index of publications available, write to the U.S. State Department, Bureau of Consular Affairs, Washington, D.C. 20520. Ask for the publication entitled, *User Guide to Bureau of Consular Affairs Automated Fax System.*

» Computer information services such as *CompuServe* or *Prodigy* carry Consular Information Sheets and Travel Warnings. You can also find them on the Internet.

» Check with your travel agent. They often can access State Department travel information through their computer systems.

Free Publications From The State Department

Single copies of the following brochures can be obtained free by sending a self-addressed, stamped envelope to: CA/PA, Room 5807, Department of State, Washington, D.C. 20520-4818.

Crisis Abroad-What the State Department Does

The Citizens Emergency Center

Consuls Help Americans Abroad

Single copies of the following information sheets are also free and can be obtained by sending a self-addressed, stamped envelope to: CA/OCRs/CCS, Room 4817, Department of State, Washington, D.C. 20520-4818.

Dual Nationality (U.S./Other)

Loss of U.S. Citizenship

Marriage Abroad

Foreign Military Service

Claims to Inheritance Abroad

Estates Abroad

Tourist and Trade Complaints

State Department Publications For Sale

The State Department publishes many other publications of interest to travelers that are sold through the U.S. Government Printing Office. To obtain a copy of any of the following publications write to

Superintendent of Documents, U.S. Government Printing Office, Washington, D.C., 20402. You can also order by telephone at (202) 783-3238. Be sure to enclose the correct amount with your order. The prices shown are subject to change.

Your Trip Abroad, $1.25

A Safe Trip Abroad, $1

Key Officers of Foreign Service Posts, $3.75

Travel Tips for Older Americans, $1

Tips for Americans Residing Abroad, $1

Background Notes. Brief pamphlets on each country of the world, one for each country. Each country is $1.

Tips for Travelers Series. Pamphlets on specific areas of the world. Depending on the region, the pamphlets cover topics such as entry requirements, currency, customs regulations, import and export controls, or health. All are $1 except where shown. The following pamphlets have been issued:

Tips for Travelers to the Caribbean

Tips for Travelers to Central and South America

Tips for Travelers to Eastern Europe

Tips for Travelers to Mexico

Tips for Travelers to the Middle East and North Africa, $1.25

Tips for Travelers to the People's Republic of China

Tips for Travelers to South Asia

Tips for Travelers to Sub-Saharan Africa

Tips for Travelers to Russia

If ordering documents through the Government Printing Office, be aware that this can be a very slow method of obtaining information. Orders often take three months or longer to reach you and are often filled incorrectly or incompletely. If you live in a large city, you may have better luck getting your order filled quickly and correctly by placing the order through a U.S. Government Bookstore. Look in the U.S. Government section of your phone book under Government Printing Office, to see if there is a bookstore in your area. The bookstores may stock the publication you want, or they can order it for you.

The following publications are available from the U.S. General Services Administration. Write to Consumer Information Center-4A, P.O. Box 100, Pueblo, Colorado 81002.

*Foreign Entry Requirements, $.50

*Passports: Applying for Them the Easy Way, $.50

Part 2

Staying Healthy Abroad

Along with the joys of international travel comes an increased risk of experiencing health problems. In addition to fatigue, jet lag, new foods, and different sleep patterns, travel exposes your body to organisms for which it has no prior exposure or resistance. Also, the methods of sanitation, water purification, and food preparation in much of the world are often not up to U.S. standards. The information in these chapters is designed to help lessen your risk of becoming sick or injured during your trip. These chapters are based largely on guidance provided to international travelers by the U.S. Public Health Service and the World Health Organization.

Americans have always been eager for travel, that being how they got to the New World in the first place.
—Otto Friedrich

Chapter 12

Preparing For A Healthy Trip Abroad

What To Take

If you use prescription medications, take a supply adequate to last your entire trip. If you take unusual or narcotic prescription drugs, ask your doctor for a written statement describing your condition to prevent problems when you go through customs. Bring along a written prescription in case you need to get a refill or lose your medications abroad. Have your physician write the prescription using the drug's generic name, not the trade name. Trade names may be different overseas but drug generic names are the same. Carry the prescription form separate from the drugs. Leave all medicines, including nonprescription medicines, in their original, labeled containers, as this will also make customs processing abroad and when you return to the U.S. easier. Have your pharmacist put liquid drugs in spill-proof containers. Always carry your medications with you, not in your luggage.

It is better to bring both prescription and over-the-counter drugs with you from home. Formulations and amounts of the active ingredients for both types of drugs bought overseas may not be the same as drugs of the same name bought in the U.S.

Take an extra pair of glasses or contact lenses and the lens prescription for both your glasses and contacts. If you wear a hearing aid, bring along spare batteries.

If you have allergies, reactions to certain medications, preexisting conditions, or other unique medical problems, consider wearing a medical alert tag or carrying a card identifying your condition. You can get medical ID tags from many physicians or from the Medic Alert Foundation, P.O. Box 1009, Turlock, California 95381, (800) 344-3226. Cards identifying your medical condition can be obtained from the American Medical Association, 535 N. Dearborn Street, Chicago, Illinois 60610, or your physician.

Before leaving, put together a medical kit of over-the-counter remedies that you use or may need while traveling such as motion sickness medicine, sun screen, pain relievers, indigestion medicine, laxatives, and antihistamines. You should also pack some first aid supplies. It is often easier to bring these things from home than to find them abroad. Keep all your medications in your carry-on luggage in case your checked bags get lost or stolen. Take some type of water purifier if you will be traveling in parts of the world where the water is of questionable quality.

If You Need Medical Care Abroad

If you get sick or are injured abroad, American embassies or consulates, or travel agents can usually provide names of hospitals, doctors, dentists, or other medical specialists. They will often be able to refer you to English-speaking professionals who are familiar with U.S. medical standards and practices.

Many premium credit cards also offer, usually free of charge, an emergency traveler's assistance service that will provide the names of English-speaking medical professionals and facilities in the area you are visiting. Some will also assign a doctor or dentist from the U.S. to consult by phone with the local medical personnel attending you to monitor your treatment. They are accessed by telephone and many will accept collect calls when you are outside the U.S. If you have this service, be sure to bring the telephone number with you before you depart.

Another excellent way to find good medical care overseas is to become a member of the International Association for Medical Assistance to Travelers (IAMAT). This is a nonprofit organization designed to assist travelers who experience a medical problem while they are in a country different than their own. There is no charge for individual memberships, but most subscribers send a donation to help support this worthwhile effort. Donations are tax deductible. Members receive a membership card and a booklet listing the locations and phone numbers of IAMAT affiliated centers, hospitals, and clinics in more than 130 countries and territories. These facilities will provide members a list of English-speaking doctors who have agreed to charge you according to an approved fee schedule. For further information contact IAMAT at 417 Center Street, Lewiston, New York 14092.

If you cannot find medical help any other way and you can make an international phone call, telephone the State Department's Citizens Emergency Center, (202) 647-5225, in the United States. They can contact the nearest U.S. consul and may be able to arrange assistance or tell you how to get help.

Health Insurance

If you become ill or injured overseas, medical care can be very costly and you may not be covered by your normal health insurance. Many health insurance policies are not valid outside the U.S. **The Social Security Medicare program does not cover hospital and medical services outside of the United States.** Check your health insurance policy to be sure that it covers medical services abroad. If your health insurance policy does not cover you abroad, consider purchasing a temporary health policy that does.

Some Medicare supplemental plans will cover medical care abroad if the treatment rendered would have been eligible for coverage in the U.S. Note that the supplemental plans normally reimburse you for your expenses. You will probably have to pay the bill at the time of treatment and file a claim when you return home. Also, the supplemental plans normally have a maximum coverage amount per trip.

Even if your health insurance covers medical care abroad, consider purchasing a traveler's health and emergency assistance policy to cover medical evacuation to the United States. Medical evacuation can easily cost more than $15,000 depending on your location and condition. Most regular health insurance policies that provide international coverage will not cover medical evacuations abroad.

There are short term health insurance policies available that have been designed for international travelers. See Chapter 9 for details about travel insurance. You may or may not need traveler's health insurance, but you should review your health insurance policy and determine your needs before you depart. Whatever you choose to do about health insurance, remember to bring your policy ID card and claim forms with you.

Chapter 13

Immunizations

When people think about making an international trip, one of their first questions is often about whether they need any shots for their destination. The answer is not so simple. It depends on where you are going, how you are traveling, your health condition, your prior immunizations, and the status of diseases in the areas you will be traveling. This chapter describes how to be sure that you have received the necessary immunizations before you travel.

The terms immunization, vaccination, inoculation, and shots are used interchangeably. A vaccination exposes your immune system to a disease organism in a harmless way so that if your body is exposed to the same disease again it will be able to recognize and defend itself against infection.

In general, the risk of acquiring an illness while overseas depends on the areas of the world to be visited. Travel to developing countries places you at greater risk than travel in developed countries. In most developed countries, such as Canada, Australia, New Zealand, Japan, and the countries of Western Europe, the health risks are no greater than the risks encountered in the United States. There are exceptions to this. There is a higher risk of measles, mumps, and rubella in most of the developed world than in the U.S. In some developed countries—Germany, Ireland, Spain, Italy, Sweden, and the

United Kingdom—the risk of acquiring pertussis is greater because immunization is not as widely practiced as in the United States.

Living conditions and standards of sanitation vary considerably and immunization coverage is low in many countries in Africa, Asia, South America, Central America, Mexico, the South Pacific, Middle East, Eastern Europe, and the former Soviet Union. In these parts of the world, the risk of acquiring disease is greater, but can also vary widely. Traveling in primarily tourist locations and avoiding rural areas will lessen your risk of exposure to food or water of questionable quality. Travelers who visit small cities, villages, and rural areas off the usual tourist routes and those who have extended contact with children are at greater risk of acquiring infectious diseases. Booster or additional doses of certain vaccines and prophylactic measures are recommended for such travelers.

Required Immunizations

Most countries do not require any vaccinations for direct travel from the United States. Under World Health Organization regulations, the only disease for which any vaccination is now required for foreign travel is yellow fever, and it is only required for travel to certain countries, mostly in sub-Saharan Africa. Many countries that do not require yellow fever vaccination for travel to the country directly from the U.S. will require proof of yellow fever vaccination if you enter the country from another country where yellow fever is present.

Yellow Fever
For direct travel from the United States, the only vaccination currently required is for yellow fever and only for entry to the following countries:

South America
French Guiana

Africa
Benin
Burkina Faso
Cameroon
Central African Republic
Congo
Cote D'Ivoire
Gabon
Liberia

Mali
Mauritania-For travel of 2
   weeks or more.
Niger
Rwanda

Senegal
Sao Tome and Principe-For
   travel of 2 weeks or more.
Togo
Zaire

International Certificate of Vaccination. If a country requires yellow fever vaccination for either direct travel from the U.S. or travel from an infected area, you will need an *International Certificate of Vaccination*. This is a passport sized booklet in which your history of inoculations can be recorded. The booklet is often referred to as the "Yellow Card." You should carry this document as proof of inoculations. Keep it with your passport. Be sure it is completed fully and correctly before you leave.

Yellow fever vaccinations must be given at an official yellow fever vaccination center designated by a state health department. Other vaccinations can be given by any licensed physician. Vaccination against yellow fever is accomplished by one shot given 10 days prior to departure, with booster shots given every 10 years. When you receive a yellow fever immunization, the physician will validate your *International Certificate of Vaccination* with a "Uniform Stamp." The certificate must be properly stamped and validated to be accepted by health authorities. Health departments, vaccination centers, or travel health clinics should have the *International Certificates of Vaccination* if you do not already have one. Information on the location of yellow fever vaccination centers can be obtained from your local or state health departments.

Remember that if you travel to countries not shown above from infected areas, you may be required to obtain yellow fever immunization. Check with your state or county health department, traveler's health clinic, or the U.S. Public Health Service for current requirements since infected areas can change.

Cholera
Cholera immunization should no longer be required to enter any country. Vaccination against cholera was required in the recent past, but in 1988, the World Health Organization rescinded any requirement for cholera immunization. Cholera immunization is generally not

considered to be highly effective since the introduction of cholera cannot be prevented by vaccination and the immunization can cause some uncomfortable side effects. However, some border officials of some countries may still demand evidence of cholera vaccination before allowing you to enter, especially if you are entering from a country where cholera is active. If you plan travel in third world countries, check with a traveler's health clinic or embassies of the countries you will visit to ensure that they will not require a cholera vaccination for entry. If you need a cholera immunization it is usually given as one shot six days before departure.

Disease Outbreaks
Sometimes certain disease epidemics occur and countries can require travelers to be immunized against the particular disease before allowing entry. This would most likely happen to Americans traveling to a country directly from a third world country where a disease epidemic has occurred. Localized disease outbreaks and immunization requirements can change rapidly. Again, the best sources of up-to-date information are a traveler's health clinic, health department, or the U.S. Public Health Service.

Returning to U.S.
No vaccinations are required for your return to the United States regardless of where you have traveled.

Recommended Immunizations

The U.S. Public Health Service has developed recommendations on vaccinations and preventative measures for U.S. travelers planning to spend time in parts of the world where preventable infectious diseases are present. These vaccinations are not required by countries to gain entry, but are generally advisable to reduce your chance of contracting disease. The majority of U.S. international travelers probably do not need any additional immunizations or prophylactic measures, provided their routine immunizations are up-to-date.

The Public Health Service's Advisory Committee on Immunization Practices makes recommendations on vaccinations. Vaccinations against diphtheria, tetanus, pertussis, measles, mumps, rubella, poliomyelitis, and *Haemophilus influenzae* type b meningitis and invasive disease are routinely administered in the United States, usually in childhood. Routine vaccination against hepatitis B virus infection is now recommended for all infants. Whether or not international travel is planned, the Public Health Service recommends that immunization against the above diseases be obtained if you do not have a history of adequate protection against these diseases.

The recommended vaccinations against other diseases depends upon your specific travel itinerary and the current disease status in the areas you will visit. For instance, typhoid vaccinations are not required for international travel but are recommended for areas where there is risk of exposure. Every two weeks the Public Health Service publishes the *Summary of Health Information for International Travel* that lists the updated status of diseases and the vaccinations recommended or required worldwide. This publication is available to physicians, travel clinics, and health departments.

To be sure that you are properly vaccinated against the diseases present in the countries you will visit, at least six weeks prior to your departure, contact a physician (preferably one familiar with international travel medicine), a travel health clinic, or your local or state health department. Many health departments operate traveler's immunization clinics. These places will be able to advise you on your specific vaccination requirements, administer any recommended vaccines, and provide you an *International Certificate of Vaccination*.

Determining which immunizations you need requires knowledge of where you are going and how you are traveling along with information on health and disease conditions in the places you will be visiting. Your primary care physician may not always be the best source of immunization advice. Better are traveler's health clinics that keep up with changing worldwide health conditions and the most current Public Health Service immunization recommendations. Many state health departments run immunization and travel clinics. You can also find traveler's health clinics listed in your yellow pages under the "Physicians" heading and the "Infectious Disease" or "Travel Medicine" subheadings. You should not get immunization advice from your travel agent. They generally do not have the technical expertise nor up-to-date disease information to advise travelers about health matters. See a medical professional.

You can also obtain disease and vaccination information directly from the Public Health Service's Centers for Disease Control. The CDC operates an automated travelers' hotline, accessible from a touch-tone phone, 24 hours-a-day, 7 days-a-week. The number is (404) 332-4559. This system provides information on vaccination requirements and recommendations for the international traveler as well as recommended preventative measures. This information is also available by facsimile at (404) 332-4565.

If you arrive in a country without required immunizations you can be denied entry, be quarantined, or required to receive an immunization with a needle and syringe of uncertain sterilization. Get your immunizations in the U.S. and document them on your Yellow Card.

Allow sufficient time to complete the necessary immunizations before traveling. Sometimes different vaccinations cannot be given together. Others need to be given several times after a week or more waiting period between inoculations. Obtaining the required and recommended immunizations to travel to less developed parts of the world can take six to eight weeks to complete. You should research which vaccinations you need eight to ten weeks before departure.

Chapter 14

Prevention And Precautions

AIDS

AIDS and the virus that causes the disease—the HIV virus—are found throughout the world. The number of persons infected with HIV worldwide is estimated by the World Health Organization to be 13 to 14 million and the disease is found in virtually every country. Because AIDS and HIV are globally distributed, the risk of AIDS to the international traveler is determined less by the destination and more by the traveler's personal behavior.

HIV is not transmitted through casual contact, air, food, water, contact with inanimate objects, or through mosquitoes or other insects. The use of public transportation by persons with AIDS does not increase the risk of infection. HIV is transmitted through sexual intercourse, needle-sharing, and blood transfusions. The precautions you should take abroad to protect yourself from infection are similar to those taken in the U.S. You are at risk of HIV infection if you:

» Have sexual intercourse (heterosexual or homosexual) with an infected person.

» Use or allow the use of contaminated, unsterilized syringes or needles for any injections or other skin-piercing procedures, including acupuncture, use of illicit drugs, steroid injections, medical or dental procedures, ear piercing, or tattooing.

» Use infected blood, blood components, or clotting factor concentrates.

Blood Transfusions Abroad

The HIV virus can be acquired through a blood transfusion. In the United States, Australia, New Zealand, Canada, Japan, and Western Europe, the risk of acquiring HIV infection through blood transfusion has been virtually eliminated through required testing of all donated blood. However, screening blood for the HIV virus is not currently done in many developing countries. International travelers to many countries are at increased risk of receiving AIDS-tainted blood if they receive a transfusion. This is a serious problem for which all international travelers, especially those visiting less developed parts of the world, need to be aware.

Some people planning international travels have requested to have their own blood, or blood from their home country available to them in case of need. This has not been feasible because of the limited storage period of blood and the need for special storage equipment. The international shipment of blood for transfusions is practical only when handled by organizations that know how to do it, such as national blood transfusion services. When you need blood in an emergency, you need it, and the international blood shipment mechanisms will not work fast enough.

The Public Health Service and the World Health Organization give the following guidance concerning blood transfusions abroad:

» Unexpected, emergency blood transfusion is rarely required. It is needed only in situations of massive hemorrhaging as can be caused by severe trauma, gynecological and obstetric emergency, or gastrointestinal bleeding.

» Blood should be transfused only when absolutely required. This applies even more forcefully in countries where blood screening for transmissible diseases is not widely performed.

» In many cases, a patient can be resuscitated through the use of colloid or crystalloid plasma expanders instead of blood. When urgent resuscitation is necessary, the use of plasma expanders rather than blood should always be considered.

» In case of an emergency need of blood, the use of plasma expanders and urgent evacuation home may be better courses of actions than receiving a blood transfusion.

» When blood transfusion cannot be avoided, instruct the attending physician to make every effort to ensure that the blood has been screened for transmissible diseases including HIV.

» International travelers should take precautions to reduce their risk of injury while abroad and establish a plan for dealing with medical emergencies should they occur.

In addition to medical treatments, travelers should also try to avoid being treated with instruments that may not have been properly sterilized. Any instrument that pierces or breaks the skin or tissues, such as dental equipment, tattoo needles, or acupuncture needles can cause infection from HIV or other blood-borne diseases. If you must be treated with a needle or instrument try to have the item boiled for 20 to 30 minutes before use unless you have seen it come directly from an unopened, sterilized package.

Protection From Diseases Carried By Mosquitoes And Other Insects

Mosquitoes and other insects can carry diseases that can be transmitted to you through an insect bite. Malaria, yellow fever, dengue fever, and encephalitis are among the diseases transmitted by mosquitoes. Plague is transmitted by fleas; encephalitis by ticks or mosquitoes.

Although there are vaccines or prophylactic drugs against some diseases (malaria and yellow fever), it is important that travelers to areas where insect diseases are prevalent take general protective measures against insects. The effectiveness of malarial prophylaxis is variable and for many insect-carried diseases, no specific preventative measures are available.

The first principle in preventing insect-borne diseases is to try to avoid areas where the disease is present. Many insect-borne diseases are prevalent in rural areas, so avoiding rural areas when possible will offer some degree of protection. However, other diseases are carried by insects that dwell in cities and around people's homes. Many insects are active only during warm months, so simply changing your itinerary can reduce your risk of acquiring certain infections. If you cannot change where or when you go, changing when and how you are out-and-about may lessen your exposure. Many insects are most active at dawn or dusk or in the early evening. Avoiding outdoor activities during these periods can reduce your exposure. Wear long sleeved shirts, long pants and hats to minimize areas of exposed skin. Shirts should be tucked in. Insect repellent applied to clothing, shoes, tents, and mosquito nets will help protect you.

If you will be exposed to ticks or mites, pants should be tucked into socks, and boots should be worn. Try to avoid wearing shorts or sandals. At the end of an outdoor outing, inspect yourself and your clothing for ticks. You will be able to see ticks easier on light colored or white clothing. You may prevent infection if you are able to promptly remove ticks.

When your accommodations are not adequately screened or air-conditioned, you should use bed nets for protection and a better night's sleep. Tuck the bed net under the mattress and spray it with repellent. You will likely find aerosol insecticides and mosquito coils for sale in areas with mosquito problems and they can help clear your room of mosquitoes. However, some of the products sold overseas contain DDT and should be used with caution. While DDT has been banned in the U.S. since 1972, it is not banned in other parts of the world. Although no longer manufactured, DDT is still found overseas in products made from old stocks.

Insect Repellents
The Public Health Service recommends insect repellents containing Permethrin for use on clothing, shoes, bed nets, and camping gear. Permethrin treated clothing repels and kills ticks, mosquitoes, and other insects and retains these effects even after repeated washes. Scientists believe that there is very little potential for toxic effects from permethrin-treated clothing.

For a repellent for use on hair and skin, most authorities recommend repellents containing DEET (diethylmethylbenzamide) as the active ingredient. DEET repels mosquitoes, ticks, and other insects when applied to skin or clothing. Purchase DEET-containing repellents in the U.S. and look for a concentration of no more than 30%. Some repellents contain a concentration as high as 95%. Concentrations of 30% are quite effective; higher concentrations are potentially toxic. Check with your physician before using DEET on children or if you are pregnant. Of course, when using any repellent, always follow the label instructions.

Preventing Malaria

Malaria is generally considered to be the most important infectious disease in the world and the disease that poses the greatest risk to travelers in malaria infected areas. About 1,000 Americans contract malaria each year. Malaria is transmitted by the bite of an infected mosquito. Areas of the world in which travelers are at high risk for malaria include Southeast Asia, Indonesia, the Indian subcontinent, China, the Middle East, Turkey, Mexico, Haiti, Central and South America, and Africa, especially sub-Saharan Africa. Malaria is increasing worldwide.

The risk of acquiring malaria varies considerably from area to area and depends upon the time of year and type of travel. In the same location, tourists staying in air-conditioned hotels are less exposed to malaria risks than backpackers or adventure travelers. The majority of malaria cases among U.S. travelers are acquired in Africa south of the Sahara. Travelers to Africa typically spend considerable time in rural areas where the malaria risk is highest. While malaria is present in Asia and South America, typically travelers to those areas spend most of their time in urban or resort areas where risk of exposure is limited.

Malaria Symptoms
Malaria can be treated effectively early in the disease, but delaying treatment can have serious or fatal consequences. The symptoms of malaria may be mild to severe. Symptoms begin eight days to several months after exposure. You should suspect malaria if you

experience an unexplained fever, or other symptoms such as persistent headaches, shaking, sweats, muscular aching and weakness, vomiting, or diarrhea after visiting a malaria infected area.

Preventative Measures
The Public Health Service recommends that all travelers to malaria infected areas of the world use prophylactic drugs and personal protective measures to prevent malaria. Even with these measures, malaria can still be contracted. The recommendations given above under *Protecting Yourself From Diseases Carried By Mosquitoes and Other Insects* should be followed to protect yourself from malaria. That is, avoid being outdoors between dusk and dawn, use mosquito netting, wear clothes that cover most of your body, apply repellents containing DEET to exposed skin, and treat clothes, tents, and mosquito nets with a permethrin-containing insect spray.

Anti-Malaria Medications
The other major way to protect yourself from malaria is to use antimalarial pills such as chloroquine. If you will travel outside of the United States, Canada, Europe, Australia, New Zealand, Japan, or Israel, you should check with your health department or an international travel clinic to see if anti-malarial pills are recommended. There are different anti-malarial drugs. Some work in one part of the world, while in other areas, the same drug is ineffective because the organism causing malaria has become resistant to that drug. Be prepared to describe in detail your travel itinerary so the proper anti-malarial drug can be prescribed. For most drugs to be effective, you need to start taking them about two weeks before you enter a malaria infected area. Many anti-malarial drug measures call for taking the medication before, during, and after your visit to a malarial area.

Malaria Information
The recommended preventative drugs change regularly because of malaria parasite resistance. Check with your physician, a travel clinic, or your local health department for current prophylactic drug recommendations. You can also get detailed recommendations from the U.S. Public Health Service, Centers for Disease Control. Call the Malaria Hotline at (404) 332-4555, available 24 hours a day.

Protection From Diseases Found In Water And Beverages

Water and beverages contaminated by viruses and bacteria are a common source of disease. Some diseases transmitted in water are bacillary dysentery, giardiasis, hepatitis A, cholera, and typhoid fever. Water that has been adequately chlorinated will provide protection against bacterial and most water-borne diseases. However, chlorine treatment alone will not kill some viruses or parasites such as the organism that causes giardiasis. In areas where chlorinated tap water is not available, or where hygiene or sanitation are poor, you should drink only the following beverages:

» Beverages made with boiled water, such as tea and coffee
» Canned or bottled carbonated beverages, such as bottled water and soft drinks. International brands of carbonated beverages are considered to be the safest.
» Beer and wine

Where water may be contaminated, remember that ice and containers for drinking should also be considered contaminated and should be avoided. Avoid using ice in beverages in these areas. It is safer to drink directly from a can or bottle than from a potentially contaminated glass. However, water on the outside of cans or bottles might also be contaminated. Wet cans or bottles should be dried before opening. Can or bottle surfaces that directly contact your mouth should first be wiped clean. You should avoid brushing your teeth with tap water if the water might be contaminated.

Treating Water
Boiling is by far the most reliable method to make water of uncertain purity safe for drinking. Bring water to a vigorous boil and then allow it to cool to room temperature. Do not add ice to cool—you will just recontaminate it. For extra safety at high altitudes, boil water for several minutes or use chemical disinfection. Where you have electricity available, bring an immersion electric coil heater to boil water. These are the devices that will boil a cup's worth of water. They are small, light, and very handy for sterilizing water. Remember to also bring the proper electric current adaptor for the country you are visiting or the heater will be useless.

Chemical disinfection with iodine is an alternative method of water treatment. Iodine tablets are available at pharmacies or sporting goods and backpacking stores. Follow the instructions on the label. If the water is cloudy, double the number of tablets. If the water is extremely cold, try to warm it up. Iodine is most effective after being in the water for eight hours. To have water available the next day, mix iodine and water at night. You can also use chlorine if boiling or iodine are unavailable, but it is not nearly as effective. Chlorine does not kill all parasites. Both iodine and chlorine will change the taste of water.

Cloudy water should first be strained through a clean cloth to remove any sediment or floating matter. Then the water should be treated with heat or iodine.

There are a variety of portable water filters on the market that the manufacturers say will provide safe drinking water. Many backpackers have used them for years with success. However, there is inconclusive scientific research on whether the filters are effective against water-borne pathogens. The Centers for Disease Control make no recommendations one way or the other regarding their use.

As a last resort, if you cannot obtain a safe source of drinking water, tap water that is uncomfortably hot to the touch is usually safe to drink. Let it cool first to room temperature in a thoroughly cleaned container.

Protection From Food-Borne Diseases

To avoid illness through your food, select what you eat with care. All raw food could be contaminated. Especially in areas where hygiene and sanitation are poor, you should avoid salads, uncooked vegetables, and unpasteurized milk and milk products such as cheese and ice cream. Eat only food that has been cooked and is still hot, or fruit that you have peeled. Under cooked and raw meat, fish, and shellfish can carry intestinal pathogens. Be sure all animal products are well cooked. Cooked food that has been allowed to stand at room temperature for several hours probably has grown bacteria and should be thoroughly reheated before serving. Sauces and mayonnaise left standing are notorious for causing food-borne disease.

Travelers' Diarrhea

Travelers' diarrhea (TD) is an all too frequent malady of the international traveler. As many as 20 to 50 percent of American travelers to several regions of the world report being afflicted. Areas for which you are at high risk for developing travelers' diarrhea include most of the developing countries of Latin America, Africa, the Middle East, and Asia. Intermediate risk destinations are most of the Southern European countries and a few Caribbean islands. Low risk destinations include Canada, Northern Europe, Australia, New Zealand, and most Caribbean islands.

Symptoms

Symptoms of travelers' diarrhea are frequent unformed bowel movements usually in combination with abdominal cramps, nausea, bloating, urgency, fever, and malaise. Symptoms usually last for 3 to 4 days, rarely more than one week. Persistent diarrhea is often the sign of some other problem, although travelers may experience more than one attack of TD during a single trip. Rarely is TD life-threatening (though when you have it you may disagree!).

Contracting TD

TD is acquired through ingesting fecally contaminated food or water that contains organisms for which the traveler's digestive system is not accustomed. Both cooked and uncooked food can cause the illness if the food is improperly handled. Especially risky foods include raw meat, raw seafood, and raw fruits and vegetables. Tap water, ice, and unpasteurized milk or other dairy products can also carry the organisms causing TD. Food purchased from street vendors has been found to cause the greatest risk of TD. Beverages generally considered safe are bottled carbonated beverages (especially flavored beverages), beer, wine, hot coffee or tea, or water boiled or properly treated with iodine or chlorine.

Prevention

There are no vaccines available that are effective against TD. Close attention to food and beverage preparation will lessen your risk, but most travelers find it difficult to avoid eating all the potential foods that can expose them to TD.

Drugs containing difenoxine (Lomotil) have been recommended for the prevention of TD. However, the Public Health Service has found that use of this drug actually increases the incidence of TD in addition to having other undesirable side effects. The use of drugs that restrict intestinal cramping (e.g. Lomotil and Imodium) were also found to be ineffective in preventing TD. There is no evidence that the use of activated charcoal prevents TD.

Bismuth subsalicylate (the active ingredient of Pepto-Bismol) taken in doses of 2 oz. four times daily or 2 tablets four times daily, has decreased the incidence of diarrhea by about 60% in several controlled studies. There are some side effects and there is not yet enough research to determine if the use of Pepto-Bismol over a period of more than three weeks is harmful. The Public Health Service has concluded that Bismuth subsalicylate appears to be an effective travelers' diarrhea preventative measure, but they do not recommend its use for more than three weeks. There are some people who should not take this medication such as pregnant women, those with ulcers, individuals with aspirin allergies, or people taking salicylates for arthritis. Check with your doctor before using Pepto-Bismol as a travelers' diarrhea preventative measure.

There are also several antimicrobial drugs that have been used to prevent TD. Antimicrobial drugs have also been shown to shorten the length of a TD illness. Because of side effects, the Public Health Service does not recommend their use as a preventative measure. Discuss these drugs with your physician so that you clearly understand the risks and benefits before using antimicrobial drugs to prevent travelers' diarrhea.

Treatment
Most cases of travelers' diarrhea will clear up on their own and require only the replacement of fluids and salts. You can achieve this best by using an oral rehydration solution such as World Health Organization Oral Rehydration Salts (ORS). This solution can be used to treat as well as prevent dehydration. ORS packets are available at stores or pharmacies in almost all developing countries. It is easily prepared; just add one packet to boiled or treated water.

Swimming Precautions

Swimming or otherwise entering bodies of water in much of the world is considered unsafe. Swimming in contaminated water can result in skin, eye, ear, and intestinal infections, especially if you submerge your head. Generally, only pools that contain chlorinated water should be considered safe places to swim. In other places you will have to use your judgment. Swimming in the developed world is generally safer than doing so in developing countries. Swimming at tropical ocean beaches away from human settlements is probably safe while swimming in a village canal is probably not. You should avoid beaches that might be contaminated with human sewage or with animal wastes.

Wading or swimming should be avoided in freshwater streams, lakes, and canals that might be infested with the snail hosts of a disease called schistosomiasis. Free-swimming larvae that live off the snail can infest fresh water, penetrate the unbroken skin of swimmers or waders, and enter the body. Schistosomiasis is a health hazard for travelers who enter fresh water in areas of the Caribbean, South America, Africa, and Asia. Countries where the disease is most prevalent include Brazil, St. Lucia, Egypt, most of sub-Saharan Africa, Southern China, the Philippines, Southeast Asia, and also Puerto Rico. Since there is no practical way to distinguish infested from non-infested water, fresh water swimming in rural areas of countries where schistosomiasis is present should be avoided.

Driving Injuries

The major cause of unexpected health problems experienced by travelers abroad is not infectious diseases. Injuries, particularly those caused by motor vehicle crashes, are the leading cause of death and disability. Driving conditions abroad are often more hazardous than found in the U.S. Depending upon your destination, hazardous roads, poor vehicle conditions, unskilled or inexperienced drivers, or drivers impaired by alcohol or drugs can contribute to hazardous driving conditions.

Driving defensively is the best preventative measure. Always try to ride or drive in vehicles with safety belts. When you rent a car insist on one with belts. A high proportion of crashes abroad occur at night, so avoid nonessential night driving. Unlit roads are commonly used at night by pedestrians, farmers and their animals, and party goers. Pedestrian, bicycle, or motorcycle travel is often dangerous in the poorly regulated traffic found in developing countries. Use a helmet for any bicycle or motorcycle travel.

Cruise Ship Sanitation

The Centers for Disease Control and the cruise ship industry jointly operate the Vessel Sanitation Program. The goal of this program is to maintain sanitation aboard cruise ships so that the risk of gastrointestinal diseases is decreased. Every vessel carrying 15 or more passengers and calling on foreign ports is inspected twice a year. You can obtain a copy of the most recent sanitation report on an individual vessel or a report of all vessel inspections, known as *The Summary of Sanitation Inspections of International Cruise Ships*, by writing to: Chief, Vessel Sanitation Program, National Center for Environmental Health, 1015 North America Way, Suite 107, Miami, FL 33132.

Post-Travel Illnesses

Some diseases do not show symptoms immediately. If you become ill after you return home, be sure to tell your physician where you have traveled. Most people who acquire an infection abroad become sick within six weeks after returning home. Some diseases can take longer. For instance, malaria may not cause symptoms for six months to a year after a traveler returns to the U.S. You should always tell your physician of the countries you visited during the 12 months preceding any illness. This information will help your doctor make the correct diagnosis.

If you become ill after returning from a trip to a third world country, consider seeing a physician specializing in international travel medicine or infectious diseases instead of, or in addition to, your regular physician. Most U.S. doctors rarely, if ever, see or treat the diseases prevalent in third world countries and may not be up-to-date on tropical medicine. Some physicians specialize in travel medicine or infectious diseases. If you think you may have contracted a tropical disease, it might be wise to see a doctor who has experience with such conditions.

Part 3

Coming Home

The next chapters contain the information returning international travelers need to help their reentry to the United States go smoothly.

When you return to the U.S., your luggage, belongings, person, or travel documents may be checked by inspectors from one or more Federal agencies. All U.S. travelers returning to the country from a trip abroad are subject to inspection at their port of entry. A port of entry is a location where people or things enter the United States. It can be an airport, a land border crossing, or a seaport.

The Federal agencies you could encounter when returning to the United States are the U.S. Immigration and Naturalization Service, the U.S. Customs Service, the Department of Agriculture's Animal and Plant Health Inspection Service, and the Public Health Service. In the major ports of entry, such as large international airports, inspectors from each of the federal agencies are assigned. In smaller ports of entry, you will always find an inspector from at least one of these agencies, most likely a Customs inspector. The inspectors present at ports of entry enforce all U.S. entry laws, not just the particular laws assigned to the particular agency. Thus, a Customs inspector can deal with immigration matters if no Immigration inspector is available.

Following are the major responsibilities in the area of international travel assigned to the four Federal agencies.

- » Immigration Service—Controls the entry of people into the United States.
- » Customs Service—Controls the entry of things such as cargo, merchandise, personal belongings, and illegal drugs into the United States.
- » Animal and Plant Health Inspection Service—Works to prevent the introduction of animal and plant diseases into the United States by controlling things that can carry disease from entering the country.
- » Public Health Service—Works to protect the public health by preventing the introduction of human diseases into the United States.

If you return to the U.S. by air or sea you will be charged a Federal inspection fee to help cover the costs of inspection by the U.S. Customs and Immigration Services. The fee is added to the price of your ticket by your carrier, travel agent, or tour operator. The fee is $10 per passenger for air or sea arrivals from most areas of the world and $6.50 for arrivals from Mexico, Canada, and the Caribbean. Until 1994, passengers arriving by air or sea from Mexico, Canada, or the Caribbean were exempt from the inspection fee. Travelers entering the U.S. from Canada and Mexico through a land border crossing do not pay an inspection fee.

What is more agreeable than one's home?
—Marcus Tullius Cicero

Chapter 15

U.S. Immigration & The Returning Traveler

When you first return to the United States through a large port of entry, the first individual you are likely to encounter will be an Immigration inspector. The Immigration inspector is interested in determining whether travelers can be legally admitted into the United States. Returning travelers establish that they can be admitted by showing proof of U.S. citizenship or resident alien status. If a passport was required for your trip, have it ready when you go through Immigration. Even if you did not need a passport to visit another country, such as travel to Canada or Mexico, be sure that you can adequately prove your identity and nationality when you pass through U.S. Immigration.

Your U.S. passport will be your best proof of citizenship and will establish that you can be readmitted to the U.S. The Immigration inspector may run your passport through a computer check to verify that it is valid, that it has not been reported lost or stolen, and that you are not wanted by any law enforcement agencies. Assuming that you have a valid U.S. passport, you should be admitted without problem and sent for Customs clearance.

If you do not have a passport, one or more of the following documents can be used to prove your citizenship.

» Certified copy of your birth certificate
» Certificate of Naturalization
» Certificate of Citizenship
» Report of Birth Abroad of a Citizen of the U.S.

Your driver's license or a government ID card with your photograph proves your identity but not your citizenship. That is not to say that you will not be readmitted back into the U.S. if you do not have a passport or one of the proofs of citizenship shown above. You probably will be admitted, but you may find you have more difficulty and have to convince the Immigration inspector that you truly are a U.S. citizen or resident alien.

Chapter 16

Clearing U.S. Customs

The U.S. Customs Service is responsible for enforcing laws that regulate the things that people bring into the country. In terms of international travel, Customs is interested in two major areas:

» Keeping things that travelers cannot bring into the U.S. out of the country.
» Collecting duty when it is owed on things travelers can bring into the U.S.

When you reenter the country you may be questioned by a Customs inspector about your trip and what you are bringing into the U.S. You or your luggage may be physically inspected by a Customs inspector, dog, or x-ray machine.

The Declaration

Returning international travelers are required to state, or "declare," to U.S. Customs anything brought back from overseas. When you return to the United States by air or sea you will be given a declaration form. Usually when you enter through a land border, you will only be asked to make an oral declaration. You must declare, either on the written form or orally, all the items that you acquired abroad that you are carrying back to the U.S. with you. The head of a family can make a joint declaration for the entire family if all of the family members live together and return to the U.S. together.

When you return from an international trip, you must declare all of the following items:

» Things that you purchased overseas
» Gifts you received overseas
» Things you bought in duty-free shops
» Repairs or alterations made to anything that you took abroad
» Anything that you are bringing home for another person
» Anything you acquired overseas that you intend to sell or use in your business

For every item that you purchased abroad, you need to write the price paid for the item on the declaration form. The price can be shown in U.S. currency or the currency of the country in which you bought the item. Keep receipts for any purchases made abroad to help prove the value of items you buy. If an item was not purchased, such as a gift you received, you should be able to give an estimate of its fair market value in the country in which the item was acquired. The declaration you make is used by Customs inspectors to determine if you owe duty, and how much, on articles brought into the U.S.

If you misrepresent items or understate their value on the declaration form, you may have to pay a penalty in addition to the payment of duty. In some cases the article can be seized by Customs. Inspectors do not rely solely on receipts you provide to determine the value of items you import. They see the articles that Americans bring into the country every day so it is likely they know the approximate value of commonly purchased items. They also use other reference materials that show the value of items sold overseas.

If you completely fail to declare an article that you acquired abroad and it is found, the article can be seized and forfeited to Customs. You may also have to pay a penalty up to the value of the article in the U.S. and you can be prosecuted. If you are not sure whether an article should be declared, declare it anyway. Let the Customs inspector tell you that your declaration was not necessary. If you are in doubt about the value of an article, declare the actual price that you paid.

Exemptions From Duty

Duty is a type of tax that countries impose on items imported into a country. U.S. residents are required to pay duty on items that they acquire overseas and bring into the U.S. However, the government allows each returning U.S. resident a certain exemption from paying duty on items they obtain abroad. The amount of the exemption you are allowed depends on where you traveled, how long you stayed, and how often you travel overseas. Family members traveling together and making a joint declaration can combine their personal exemptions to create a larger exemption even if only one family member purchased any items (except at the $200 exemption level). Children returning to the United States receive the same exemptions as adults except for exemptions on alcoholic beverages.

Exemption Levels
There are four exemption levels: $400, $600, $1200, and $200.

$400 Exemption. In most cases, you will be allowed to bring back to the U.S. free of any duty, articles that added together are $400 or less in value. The $400 exemption is based on the fair market value in the country where each item was acquired. Special rules apply to liquor, cigarettes, and cigars. Travelers can receive the $400 exemption only once in a 30 day period.

To be eligible for the $400 duty exemption, all of the following must apply:

» You acquired the articles for your personal or household use.
» You carry the articles with you when you return to the U.S.
» You are returning from a stay abroad of at least 48 hours.
» You have not used the $400 exemption, or any part of it, during the preceding 30 days.
» You properly declare the articles to Customs.
» The articles you are bringing back are not restricted or prohibited from entering the U.S.

No more than 100 cigars and 200 cigarettes (one carton) can be included in this exemption. Each returning traveler can receive the cigar and cigarette exemption regardless of age. Yes, kids too! Go figure. One liter (33.8 oz.) of alcohol can be included in the $400 exemption if you are 21 years of age or older, the liquor is for your own use, and bringing the liquor into the state in which you arrive is allowed.

$600 Exemption. If you are returning from certain countries in the Caribbean and Central America you are allowed a $600 exemption from duty. The same rules shown above for the $400 exemption also apply here. There are currently 24 countries to which this exemption applies. They are:

Antigua and Barbuda	Haiti
Aruba	Honduras
Bahamas	Jamaica
Barbados	Montserrat
Belize	Netherlands Antilles
Costa Rica	Nicaragua
Dominica	Panama
Dominican Republic	St. Christopher/Kitts and Nevis
El Salvador	Saint Lucia
Grenada	St. Vincent and the Grenadines
Guatemala	Trinidad and Tobago
Guyana	Virgin Islands, British

$1200 Exemption. If you return directly or indirectly from American Samoa, Guam, or the U.S. Virgin Islands you receive an exemption from duty on $1200 worth of merchandise. All the rules shown under the $400 exemption also apply to this exemption.

$200 Exemption. You may not always meet the criteria for the $400, $600, or $1200 exemptions, but you are always eligible for the $200 exemption. If you claimed any of the above exemptions within the preceding 30 days or if you did not stay out of the U.S. for at least 48 hours, you are not eligible for the higher exemptions. You are eligible for a $200 exemption. (Until late 1994, this exemption level was just $25.) This exemption allows you to bring in duty-free, articles with a total retail value of less than $200. If you bring back articles that value more than $200, none of your merchandise is exempted from duty. The $200 exemption applies only to individuals. It cannot be grouped by family members on one Customs declaration to create a larger exemption as can be done with the other exemption levels. This exemption can include 50 cigarettes, 50 cigars, or 150 ML (4 oz.) of liquor or alcoholic perfume.

Exemption Rules

You can combine the above exemptions if your travels take you to countries with different exemption levels. For instance, if you traveled to the U.S. Virgin Islands and the Bahamas, you can bring in $1200 worth of merchandise duty-free. Of this amount, up to $600 worth of merchandise can be from the Bahamas.

The above exemptions are not cumulative. You cannot save up an unused exemption amount from one trip and apply it to a subsequent trip. For example, if you are entitled to a $400 exemption from a trip, but only use $100, you cannot apply the remaining $300 exemption to a trip you take two weeks later. You need to wait 30 days between trips before you receive another $400 exemption.

Rates Of Duty

So how much will you have to pay in duty if you come back to the U.S. with merchandise worth more than the amount of your duty exemption? It depends. There is a flat rate of duty and variable rates of duty that are calculated based on how much you bought and where you bought the items. Any merchandise that you bring into the U.S. that is worth more than your Customs exemption is subject to duty. Remember that family members can pool exemptions except for the $200 exemption.

First the Customs inspector will determine which of the items you acquired abroad have the highest rates of duty and will apply their value against your exemption. Then your exemption level ($400, $600, $1200, but not $200) will be deducted and you will be charged no duty on articles up to that amount. A flat rate of duty is then applied to the next $1000 worth of merchandise. The flat duty rate is 10% for most countries and 5% for items acquired in the U.S. Virgin Islands, American Samoa, or Guam. Variable duty rates are then charged for any merchandise worth more than your exemption and the first $1000 level. At this level the duty rates vary by product and the product's country of origin. Most countries have been granted *Most Favored Nation Status* which permits merchandise from those countries to enter the U.S. at a lower duty rate than merchandise from nations without the status. You can be pretty sure that the countries you will visit will have Most Favored Nation Status, but the status can change so check with Customs if in doubt.

Here are the rates of duty (for Most Favored Nation Status countries) for some items that Americans commonly purchase overseas. Remember that these rates are charged only when you return with merchandise worth more than your personal exemption and $1000. The first $1000 of merchandise over your personal exemption is charged duty at the flat 10% rate.

Antiques—Items made at least 100 years before the date of entry to the U.S. are admitted duty free.

Bone China Tableware	8%
Cameras	
Video	4.5%
Still	3%
Lenses	6.6%
Chess Sets	4.6%
China Figurines	9%
Crystal	6% to 20%
Furniture	
Wood chairs	3.4% to 5.3%
Furniture other than chairs	2.5%
Jade	
Cut but not set	2.1%
All other jade	21%
Jewelry	
Silver	27.5%
All other	6.5%
Leather Hand Bags	5.3% to 10%
Perfume	5%
Shoes	2.5% to 20%
Shell Articles	3.4%
Stones, cut but not set	
Diamonds	None
Others	None to 2.1%
Toys	7%
Watches	3.9% to 14%
Wearing Apparel	
Cotton knit	7.9% to 21%
Linen	3% to 12%
Silk	3% to 7.5%
Wool Sweaters	7.5% to 17%
Wood Carvings	5.1%

Payment Of Duty

Welcome back to the U.S. Now pay up! If you owe duty, you will have to pay it upon your arrival. For payment of duty, the Customs Service accepts:

- » U.S. currency. Foreign currency is not accepted.
- » Personal checks drawn on a U.S. bank.
- » Money orders or traveler's checks as long as they do not exceed the amount of duty by more than $50.
- » Some, but not all locations, will accept VISA, MasterCard, or Discover credit cards.

GSP Duty Exemptions For Developing Countries

In an attempt to boost the economies of several "developing" nations, the U.S. Government has exempted from duty some products that Americans purchase from those countries. The system is called Generalized System of Preferences, or GSP. In effect, GSP allows you to import duty-free, a wide range of products from many countries for which you would otherwise have to pay duty.

The items exempted include many luxury items such as precious and semiprecious stones, jewelry, and furniture. The list of developing countries and territories is extensive; there are over 125 countries to which the GSP exemption applies. Countries not usually considered "developing" such as some Caribbean nations and Israel are considered developing countries for GSP purposes.

To take advantage of GSP, you must have purchased an eligible item that was grown, manufactured, or produced in an eligible country. You can bring the item with you on your return, or you can ship it directly from the developing country to the U.S.

GSP Eligible Products

Over 4,000 items are eligible for duty-free entry from the designated developing countries. Footwear, most clothing, watches, some electronic products, glass, and steel products are excluded from

GSP benefits. Below is a list of some popular items Americans purchase abroad that can generally be brought back to the U.S. duty-free if the item comes from an eligible country. Sometimes certain of the items shown from certain countries may be excluded from eligibility.

Baskets or bags of bamboo, willow, rattan
Cameras–Motion-picture and still, lenses, other photo equipment
Candy
Chinaware
    Bone: household ware, vases, statues, figurines
    Non-bone: articles other than household ware
Cork products
Earthenware or stoneware
Furniture of wood, rattan, or plastic
Games played on boards such as chess sets
Golf equipment and balls
Jade–cut but not set for use in jewelry and other jade articles
Jewelry of precious metal or precious stones, or of precious metal set with semiprecious stones, cameos, intaglios, amber, or coral. Necklaces and neck chains made almost wholly from gold, except rope from Israel and mixed link.
Jewelry boxes if unlined
Music boxes
Musical instruments
Paper products
Pearls–cultured or imitation, loose or temporarily strung and without a clasp
Perfume
Printed matter
Radio receivers
Records–phonographs or tapes
Shell products
Silver tableware and flatware
Skis and ski equipment, but not ski boots
Stones–cut but not set, suitable for use in jewelry. Includes precious and semiprecious stones, coral, and cameos.
Tape recorders
Toys
Wigs
Wood carvings

Remember, this is just a partial list of GSP eligible items. There are more than 4,000 eligible products. Check with U.S. Customs before you leave or the American consulate or embassy in the country you are visiting to verify the GSP status of any article you are considering bringing to the U.S.

Eligible Countries
Following are the GSP eligible countries and territories. When you purchase GSP eligible items from these countries, you can bring the items into the U.S. duty-free.

Albania	Costa Rica	Jordan
Angola	Cote D'Ivoire	Kenya
Antigua & Barbuda	Croatia	Kiribati
Aruba	Cyprus	Latvia
Argentina	Czech Republic	Lebanon
Bahamas	Djibouti	Lesotho
Bahrain	Dominica	Lithuania
Bangladesh	Dominican Rep.	Macau
Barbados	Ecuador	Madagascar
Belize	Egypt	Malawi
Benin	El Salvador	Malaysia
Bhutan	Equatorial Guinea	Maldives
Bolivia	Estonia	Mali
Bosnia-Herzegovina	Ethiopia	Malta
Botswana	Fiji	Mauritius
Burundi	French Polynesia	Montserrat
Brazil	Gambia	Mexico
Bulgaria	Ghana	Morocco
Burkina Faso	Grenada	Mozambique
Cameroon	Guatemala	Namibia
Cape Verde	Guinea Bissau	Nepal
Cayman Islands	Guyana	Netherland Antilles
Central African Republic	Haiti	Niger
	Honduras	Oman
Chad	Hungary	Pakistan
Chile	India	Palau
Columbia	Indonesia	Papua New Guinea
Comoros	Israel	Paraguay
Congo	Jamaica	Peru

Philippines	Solomon Islands	Turks and Caicos
Poland	Somalia	Islands
Rwanda	Sri Lanka	Tuvalu
St. Kitts and Nevis	Sudan	Uganda
St. Lucia	Surinam	Uruguay
St. Vincent and the Grenadines	Swaziland	Vanuatu
	Tanzania	Venezuela
Sao Tome and Principe	Thailand	Virgin Islands
	Togo	Western Samoa
Senegal	Tonga	Yemen
Seychelles	Trinidad & Tobago	Zaire
Sierra Leone	Tunisia	Zambia
Slovakia	Turkey	Zimbabwe
Slovenia		

If you plan to do any extensive shopping in any of the countries shown above request the leaflet, *GSP & The Traveler*, from your nearest Customs office, or write to U.S. Customs Service, P.O. Box 7407, Washington, D.C. 20044.

Personal Belongings Taken Abroad

You could be charged duty on foreign made personal belongings that you take abroad each time you bring them back into the United States unless you can prove that you possessed the items prior to your departure. To avoid being forced to pay duty on articles that were bought in the U.S., be prepared to prove that the purchases were made in this country. Documents that fully describe the article such as a bill of sale, insurance policy, jeweler's appraisal, or receipt for purchase are usually accepted as proof of prior possession.

Items that have permanent serial numbers such as foreign made cameras and watches can be taken to your local customs office and registered before departure. You will receive a *Certificate of Registration*. Carry this document when you travel abroad with foreign made articles and you should be able to easily reenter these items duty-free. Keep the certificate as it is valid for any subsequent foreign trips you make. Unfortunately, you cannot register items by mail or phone. A Customs officer must physically inspect your items. You can also register foreign made valuables with Customs at the airport when you depart, but allow extra time to do so and be sure a Customs officer is on duty when you are departing.

Gifts

People traveling abroad often ship merchandise to the U.S. as gifts for friends and relatives. If you ship gifts to the U.S., do not declare these shipments when you reenter the country. You only declare items that you hand-carry on your return.

With the exception of alcohol and cigarettes, legitimate gifts up to $100 in retail value that you ship to an individual in the U.S. can be received by that person free of duty. The individual can receive no more than $100 in gift shipments per day or $200 per day for shipments received from the U.S. Virgin Islands, American Samoa, or Guam. The recipient must pay duty on shipments valued at more than these amounts. You, as a traveler, cannot legally send a "gift" to yourself nor can persons traveling together send gifts to each other to avoid paying duty. You are supposed to pay duty on any items that you mail to yourself from abroad.

To expedite a shipped gift through Customs mark the outside of the package as "Unsolicited Gift," and include your name, the name of the recipient, the nature of the gift(s), and the retail value of each gift. Many foreign post offices will provide a form for this purpose.

Gifts that you carry back to the U.S. are considered by Customs to be for your personal use and are subject to duty. They may be included in your duty exemption. This includes both gifts that were given to you by others while abroad and gifts that you plan to give to others in the U.S. Merchandise that you intend to use as gifts for business purposes may be exempt. Check with Customs when you reenter.

Mailing Or Shipping Items Home

You are allowed an exemption from duty, normally $400, only on foreign merchandise that you carry with you on your return to the U.S. Many people decide to ship home items purchased abroad instead of lugging them around during their travels. Items that you purchase abroad and mail or ship home to yourself cannot be included in your exemption when you return. All shipped items are subject to duty when received in the U.S. with no duty exemption allowed. The only exception is gifts you ship to someone else with a value of $100 or less, as described above.

The Postal Service sends all foreign mail packages arriving in the U.S. to a Customs Service international mail facility before making delivery. A Customs inspector examines the parcel, which may include opening it, and determines if any duty is owed. If no duty is owed, the package is returned to the Postal Service for delivery to you without any additional postage or handling charges. If duty is owed, Customs will document the front of the package showing the amount of duty to be charged and return the package to the Postal Service. The duty and a postal handling fee will be collected from you by the Postal Service when they deliver your package. You will also be charged a $5 processing fee by Customs.

Some items that you ship to the U.S. may require a process called *formal entry* before being released to you. Shipped items such as some textiles, wearing apparel, and small leather goods are subject to formal entry regardless of their value or quantity. Formal entry requires the filing of the proper forms and payment of duty in order for you to obtain your merchandise. Customs employees will not prepare this type of entry for you. Only you or a licensed customs broker can prepare a formal entry. Formal entry only applies to certain items that you ship to the U.S. It does not apply if the items accompany you when you return home.

You can also ship merchandise from abroad through various shipping, air freight, and express delivery companies. When you do so, the items must clear Customs before being delivered to you. The shipping or delivery company usually accomplishes the Customs clearance of the merchandise for you. They normally charge a fee for this service.

Returning To The U.S.—Tips For Travelers

Carry Only Your Own Bags
Never carry someone else's baggage when you clear Customs—especially a stranger's. The bags and their contents will be considered to be yours, and you will be held responsible for any violations found inside. You could even experience problems carrying a friend's or tour partner's bag. The Customs inspector may want to see receipts or find out how you acquired certain items, and you probably will

not have the answers. If you do carry someone else's bags, know what is inside and have the receipts.

Proving the Value of Your Purchases
Be prepared to prove the value of your purchases when you go through Customs. Keep all evidence of your purchases made overseas such as sales slips and invoices. Store these papers together in an easily accessible location. Evidence of your purchases will be helpful when filling out your Customs declaration and for showing to the inspector to prove how much you paid for your purchases.

Packing Your Bags
Whenever you return to the U.S., you or your baggage can be inspected. The chances are you will not be inspected, but you do not know until you have cleared Customs. Make it easier on yourself and the inspector so that if you are examined you can be on your way as soon as possible. Pack your baggage in a way that will make an inspection easier. It will help if you pack all the items that you acquired overseas in one bag. Then you can quickly locate the items without opening up and fumbling through all your baggage. Appearing organized and familiar with Customs regulations may help speed you through the process.

California Residents
California residents should be aware that merchandise purchased abroad and brought back to California may be subject to a use tax. Beginning in October 1990, California began assessing a use tax on foreign purchases using information from the Customs declarations completed by returning travelers. The use tax rate is the same as the sales tax rate in the traveler's California county of residence. For information about this tax, contact the California Board of Equalization's Occasional Sales Tax Unit at (916) 445-9524.

Obtaining Customs Assistance

To obtain help from Customs while in the U.S., contact a local Customs Service office. There are over 40 Customs district offices located in most major U.S. cities. For locations, look in the U.S.

Government section of your phone book under U.S. Department of Treasury, U.S. Customs Service, District Director. You may also be able to get assistance at any of the U.S. ports of entry. Virtually all ports of entry are staffed by Customs personnel. These offices will also be listed in your phone book.

You can also obtain Customs assistance in some cities abroad. Customs maintains Customs attaches at several U.S. Embassies and Consulates. Customs attaches are located in the embassies or consulates in the following cities:

Bangkok	Monterrey
Bonn	Ottawa
Dublin	Panama
The Hague	Paris
Hermosillo	Rome
Hong Kong	Seoul
London	Singapore
Merida	Tokyo
Mexico City	Vienna
Milan	

Chapter 17

Bringing Things Into The U.S.

Fakes

Many Americans purchase imitation articles abroad that have been made and labeled to look like the real thing. Examples are fake Rolex watches and Gucci handbags. It is illegal to bring these items into the U.S. and Customs will confiscate them if they find them. A great deal on a fancy fake watch could vanish. If you buy name brand merchandise overseas be sure the items are real. If you cannot be sure, or if the price is too good, it is better not to buy.

Duty-Free Shops

Articles that you buy in "duty-free" shops in foreign countries are **not** duty-free when you bring them into the U.S. These items are subject to the same Customs duty, restrictions, and exemptions that apply to any other merchandise bought overseas and brought into the country. Articles sold in duty-free shops are free of duty and taxes only for the country in which the shop is located. Articles sold in duty-free shops are for export, not for use in the country of purchase.

If you buy an item in a foreign airport's duty-free shop, the price you pay does not include the import tax you would have to pay for that same item purchased in a regular shop located in that country. When you return to the U.S., if the value of the item you bought in a duty-free shop exceeds your personal exemption, you will have to pay U.S. duty on it. Duty-free does not mean free from U.S. duty.

Money

You can bring into the U.S. as much money as you wish. However, if you enter the country with more than $10,000 in any form—cash, checks in bearer form, money orders, or traveler's checks—you have to declare to U.S. Customs that you are doing so. A check in bearer form is a negotiable check made out to cash or endorsed by the payee. You make the required declaration on Customs Form 4790, available at ports of entry. By documenting the movement of large sums of money, the government is attempting to stem the flow of money earned in the international drug trade or through other illegal activities. You can bring more than $10,000 into the country as long as you tell Customs about the money. If you do not tell Customs about a large sum of money you are carrying and they find it, they will seize the funds and you may be subject to further penalties. The same rules apply when departing the U.S. See Chapter 6.

Books, Recordings, Computer Programs, And Videos

The U.S. prohibits the importation of any copyrighted article that was produced overseas without the authorization of the copyright owner. Such products are commonly called "pirated" articles. U.S. travelers will frequently find books, recordings, movie videos, and computer programs for sale overseas at much cheaper prices than can be found in the U.S. These items have often been copied without the authorization of the book publisher, recording company, movie studio, or software maker, and therefore, were reproduced illegally. Besides often being inferior in quality, you cannot legally bring pirated items into the U.S. If the Customs Service finds that you have pirated items, they will seize and destroy them unless you can prove that you did not know the items were pirated. If that were the case, Customs will allow you to return the items to the country of origin. Either way you do not get to bring the merchandise into the U.S. Beware of buying books, records, videos, or software overseas. You may come back with nothing.

Medicine And Narcotics

It is commonly known that narcotics and other illegal drugs are prohibited from entering the U.S. and there are severe penalties if imported. U.S. Customs can fine and prosecute anyone entering the country with illegal drugs regardless of the amount. Anabolic steroids are also prohibited from entry.

While traveling, if you need to carry medicines containing habit-forming drugs or narcotics such as cough medicine, diuretics, heart drugs, tranquilizers, sleeping pills, depressants, or stimulants, you should do the following:

» Be sure all drugs are properly identified. Carry drugs in their original, labeled containers.

» Carry only an amount of the drug that would normally be carried by a person having the health problem for which the drug is prescribed.

» Have either a prescription for the drug or a written statement from your physician stating that the drug is being used under a doctor's direction and is necessary for your physical well-being while traveling.

Certain drugs and medical devices sold overseas cannot be brought into the U.S. In order to bring a drug or device into the U.S., its use in this country must be approved by the Food and Drug Administration. There are several newer or unorthodox drugs or medical devices that are legal and available overseas, but not approved for use in the U.S. The process to get newer drugs approved in the U.S. is often much longer than the process in other countries. While these drugs and devices may be completely legal elsewhere, they cannot be brought into or used in the U.S., even if the product has been prescribed for you by a foreign physician.

For further information on importing newer drugs and devices contact your nearest FDA office found in the U.S. Government section of your phone book under the Department of Health and Human Services listing, or write to: Food and Drug Administration, Import Operations Unit, Room 12-8, 5600 Fishers Lane, Rockville, Maryland 20857.

Firearms And Ammunition

Only licensed firearms importers, dealers, or manufacturers can import firearms or ammunition to the U.S. Do not bother trying to import firearms or ammunition if you are not authorized to do so. The item will be confiscated by Customs. If you find a firearm overseas that you want to bring into the U.S., such as a rare gun, you will have to arrange the importation through a licensed importer. (Also be sure that you can get an export permit before attempting to take a firearm out of a foreign country.)

You can bring firearms or ammunition back into the U.S. that you personally took out of the country. You will have to prove that you took the items out of the U.S. Before departing, go to any Customs Service office or an Alcohol, Tobacco and Firearms (ATF) field office and register the firearms or ammunition. To locate your nearest ATF office, look in the U.S. Government section of your phone book under Treasury Department. ATF offices are usually located only in larger cities. Remember that most countries will also regulate the importation of firearms or ammunition into the country. Check with the country's embassy or consulate before trying to enter with these items.

For more information on bringing firearms or ammunition into the U.S. contact the Bureau of Alcohol, Tobacco and Firearms, Department of Treasury, Washington, D.C. 20226 or a local field office.

Gold

It was formerly prohibited to import gold coins, medals, or bullion into the U.S. For the most part those restrictions have been removed. Copies of gold coins are still not allowed in unless they are properly marked.

Glazed Ceramics

Be cautious in purchasing any glazed ceramic ware abroad. Unless properly glazed, ceramics can leach lead into the food or beverage that they hold. Much of the ceramic ware sold overseas is not made to U.S. specifications. It is possible to suffer lead poisoning from consuming food or beverages that are stored or served in improperly glazed ceramics. Unless the ceramics are made by a firm with a good international reputation, there is no way to be certain, without testing, that a particular item will be safe. The Food and Drug Administration recommends that food and beverage ceramic ware purchased abroad be tested for lead release by a commercial laboratory when you return to the U.S. If you decide not to test a ceramic product obtained overseas, use the article for decorative purposes only.

Works Of Art

Works of art may be brought into the U.S. free of duty, but the item has to truly be a "work of art." What you consider to be a work of art created by a professional artist and free from duty, may be considered by Customs to be the work of a craftsman and subject to duty. To be free from duty a work of art must be original in concept, unique, and created by a professional artist. If the item is mass-produced or available from several vendors, it will not be considered a work of art, no matter how beautiful or artistic.

Antiques

Antiques can be imported duty-free. To be considered an antique, an item must have been manufactured at least 100 years before the date it is brought into the U.S. Be cautious when purchasing any antique items abroad. Some countries consider the antiques of their country to be national treasures and the "inalienable property of the nation." Foreign customs authorities will seize illegally purchased antiques. You may also be subject to a fine. It is often difficult for travelers to tell the difference between legally and illegally purchased antiques. American citizens have been arrested and prosecuted for purchasing antiques abroad. Even purchasing reproductions of antiques from street vendors is not necessarily safe. Americans have been arrested for purchasing reproductions because a local authority believed the purchase was a national treasure.

If you purchase antiques or antique reproductions, you need to protect yourself. In countries where antiques are important, obtain documentation that the antique reproduction is in fact a reproduction. If you purchase an authentic antique you must secure the necessary export permit before attempting to leave the country with the item. You may be able to get the necessary documentation or export permit through the country's national museum. A reputable dealer may also provide the export permit or tell you how to secure one.

You can obtain information on purchasing antiques from the country's tourist office. You can also consult the consular section of the U.S. Embassy or Consulate. The consular section will be aware of the local situation and any problems Americans have had in purchasing and exporting antiques or reproductions.

Trademarked Items

Many American tourists purchase items abroad that have been manufactured overseas and trademarked in the U.S. Trademarked items frequently purchased abroad include cameras, lenses, binoculars, tape recorders, musical instruments, jewelry, silverware, metalware, perfume, watches, and clocks. You may be limited in the quantity of foreign-made trademarked articles that you can bring into the U.S. You can always bring one trademarked article back for your personal use during any 30 day period. Some manufacturers allow you to bring in more than one article of their product. In those cases, you can bring back up to the number of items set by the manufacturer. If you plan to purchase several of any particular trademarked item, check with the manufacturer or U.S. Customs to determine the quantity of items that you will be allowed to import.

Chapter 18

Food, Plants, Animals, & Animal Products

Various agencies of the Federal government regulate the importation of food, animal products, plants, pets, live animals, and products made from endangered species. Some items are not allowed into the country at all while others can be imported only after meeting quarantine or other requirements. Before trying to import any animal, plant, or food, or a product made from these things, be sure that the item will be allowed into the country.

Pets And Other Live Animals

All live animals brought into the U.S. must be free of any disease that can be passed to humans or livestock. Any imported animal can be quarantined or barred from the country for health reasons. These requirements apply equally to household pets that you take out and then return to the U.S. Both the Animal and Plant Health Inspection Service (APHIS) of the U.S. Department of Agriculture and the U.S. Public Health Service regulate the entry of live animals. Before importing any pet or other live animal, also check with your state agricultural and health departments for any state restrictions on live animal imports.

Pets and other animals brought into the country will be examined at the port of entry for any sign of disease. If the animal is not in good health it will be held for an examination by a veterinarian with the expenses paid by the owner. Animals can be barred from entry to the U.S. or destroyed if they are found to be diseased. Even a pet that you have taken out of the country on an overseas trip can be denied entry or even destroyed, if it is found to be carrying a dangerous disease.

Cats
Domestic cats arriving in good health will be admitted to the country. Routine rabies vaccination for cats is not required, but is recommended by the Public Health Service. Most state and local health departments do require that imported cats be vaccinated.

Dogs
Dogs must be vaccinated against rabies at least 30 days before entering the United States. Puppies less than three months old or dogs that are coming from designated rabies free countries are exceptions. The Public Health Service designates and regularly updates the countries that are considered rabies free. Some of the rabies free countries are most Caribbean countries, Japan, Korea, Malaysia, Singapore, Taiwan, Denmark, Finland, Greece, Ireland, Norway, Portugal, Spain, Sweden, the United Kingdom, and most South Pacific countries such as Australia and New Zealand.

If the dog has come from an area that is not rabies free, you will need a valid rabies vaccination certificate before the dog will be allowed in. If you do not have a rabies vaccination certificate, you will have to vaccinate your dog and confine it for 30 days. Young puppies brought from areas that are not rabies free must be vaccinated when they reach three months of age and then confined for a 30 day period. For rabies vaccination information, contact the U.S. Public Health Service, Centers for Disease Control, Division of Quarantine, Atlanta, Georgia 30333, (404) 639-8107.

Birds
Pet birds from the U.S. that leave the country and return within 60 days can be brought back in without quarantine if the owner has a U.S. veterinary health certificate. All other birds must be quarantined for 30 days upon arrival at a USDA quarantine facility located

at seven ports of entry around the country. The cost for quarantine is about $125 per bird and is paid by the owner. Quarantine space must be reserved in advance. For information and a permit application write to: USDA, APHIS, Veterinary Services, P.O. Box 96464, Washington, D.C. 20090-6464, ATTN: National Center for Import/Export.

Food, Plants, And Animal Products

The Animal and Plant Health Inspection Service (APHIS) regulates the food, plant, and animal products that can be brought into the U.S. from foreign countries. The restrictions are designed to prevent the importation of foreign animal and plant pests and diseases that could harm U.S. crops, livestock, pets, or the environment.

When you return to the U.S., you must declare any meats, fruits, vegetables, plants, animals, or plant and animal products that you are carrying. You can make the declaration on the Customs declaration form. Many plant and animal items pose no threat to U.S. agriculture or the environment and can be imported freely. Inspectors may look in your baggage for any undeclared agricultural products. Sometimes they use dogs to sniff your luggage or x-ray machines to reveal undeclared products. If they find an undeclared product, you can be fined on the spot up to $250 and the product will be confiscated.

Fruits, Vegetables, And Plants

You can bring in some fruits, vegetables, and plants provided you have declared them and they are inspected and found to be free of pests. If you plan on growing the plant in the U.S. you will be required to get advance permission to import in most cases. For information and a permit application write to: USDA, APHIS, Plant Protection and Quarantine, P.O. Box 96464, Washington, D.C. 20090-6464, ATTN: Port Operations.

Meat and Animal Products

Fresh and dried meats and meat products cannot be imported from most countries. If any meat is used in preparing a product, it is generally prohibited. Commercially canned meat will be allowed in if the inspector can tell that the meat was cooked in the can after it was sealed. Otherwise canned meat is also prohibited. Hunting trophies, game animal carcasses, and hides are severely restricted. If you intend to bring these items into the country write to the following address for information and permit forms: USDA, APHIS, Veterinary Services, P.O. Box 96464, Washington, D.C. 20090-6464, ATTN: National Center for Import/Export.

Soil, Sand, Minerals, And Shells
Harmful organisms can live in soil and may threaten plants and animals. If you visited a farm while overseas, agricultural inspectors may want to disinfect your shoes, clothes or vehicle. You are not allowed to bring in any soil, earth, or sand with one exception; you are allowed one ounce of decorative beach sand. Rocks, minerals, and shells are allowed in, but all sand and soil must be cleaned off. Rinse rocks and shells before packing them.

Agricultural Products You Can Bring Back
The Animal and Plant Health Inspection Service has produced the following list of approved agricultural products that can be brought into the U.S. The list covers all areas of the world except Canada, Mexico, Hawaii, Puerto Rico, and the U.S. Virgin Islands. Agricultural products not on this list may still be allowed in if they are inspected and found to be free of pests or diseases.

Bamboo, dried poles only
Beads made of seeds (but not jequirity beans)
Breads, cakes, cookies, and other bakery goods
Candies
Cheeses, fully cured (but not cottage cheeses)
Coconuts (but husks or milk must be removed)
Coffee, roasted beans only
Dried foods, including polished rice, beans, tea
Fish
Flower bulbs (but not crocosomia, gladiolus and watsonia bulbs
    from Africa, Argentina, Brazil, France, Italy, Malta, Mauritius,
    Portugal, or Uruguay)
Flowers, most fresh or dried kinds (but not with roots), except
    eucalyptus
Fruits, canned or dried products only
Herbarium plants (but not witchweed)
Herbs, dried, for medicinal use
Meats, canned (but subject to the restrictions discussed above)

Mushrooms
Nuts (but not chestnuts, acorns, or nuts with outer husks)
Sauces, canned or processed
Seaweed
Seeds (but not avocado, bamboo, barberry, coconuts, corn, cotton, currant, elm, hibiscus, lentil, mahonia, mango, pearl millet, potato, rice, sorghum, or wheat)
Shamrocks, without roots or soil
Soup and soup mixes (but not those containing meat)
Spices, dried (but not curry leaves)
Straw animals, hats, baskets, and other souvenirs (but not items stuffed with straw)
Vegetables, canned or processed

Approved Products From Canada. Most products produced or grown in Canada are allowed. This includes vegetables, fruits other than black currants, and meat and dressed poultry if you can prove the origin of the product.

Approved Products From Mexico. Products brought from Mexico must have been grown or produced in Mexico. For meats, proof of origin is required. The following Mexican products can be imported.

Acorns
Bananas
Blackberries
Cactus fruits
Cerimans
Coconuts (but husks or milk must be removed)
Corn husks
Dates
Dewberries
Grapes
Limes
Lychees
Meats (but not pork or uncooked poultry)
Melons
Mexican jumping beans
Nuts
Papayas
Pineapples
Strawberries
Tamarind bean pods
Vegetables (but not potatoes, sweet potatoes or yams)

Note that if you take agricultural products of U.S. origin out of the United States, you are not always allowed to bring them back into the country when you return. It depends upon the agricultural product you are carrying and where you have traveled.

Questions About Importing Agricultural Products

You can check with APHIS before you depart if you have questions about which agricultural products can be brought back into the U.S. For the nearest office look in the U.S. Government pages of your phone book under Department of Agriculture, Animal and Plant Health Inspection Service, Plant Protection and Quarantine, or contact the national office: Animal and Plant Health Inspection Service, U.S. Department of Agriculture, Hyattsville, Maryland 20782, (301) 436-8170. You may also be able to get advice while overseas from a U.S. Embassy or Consulate about which agricultural products you can bring into the country. Consulate personnel are usually familiar with the local agricultural products for sale and the U.S. restrictions. See Appendix B for the locations of U.S. Embassies and Consulates.

Wildlife And Endangered Species Souvenirs

Be especially careful about purchasing and bringing back to the U.S. any souvenir containing animal products. Things made from animal hides, shells, feathers, and teeth are common souvenir items in marketplaces all over the world. Quite often these products are made from endangered species and it is illegal to import them into the United States. Souvenirs made of tortoise shell, coral, ivory, and reptile skin fashioned into boots, jewelry, leather goods, and knickknacks are commonly available. Just because these items are for sale in another country does not mean that you can import them into the U.S., regardless of what the seller of the item tells you. Most Americans do not realize that it is a crime to bring any endangered species souvenir into the U.S.

It is often difficult to tell whether an animal product you are considering purchasing will be legal to import to the U.S. The legality of importing wildlife products depends upon the species and the country of origin. Wildlife is often illegally killed in one country, smuggled into another, and then exported with false permits to a third, making it extremely difficult to trace its origins.

Here are some general guidelines if you are considering purchasing any souvenir made of animal products.

Reptile Skins And Leathers
These are commonly used in watchbands, belts, handbags, and shoes. You must know the species and country of origin of reptile skins or leathers before being sure that you can import them. Do not buy the following products. They are endangered and are prohibited from import.

» Sea turtle products
» Most crocodile and caiman products
» Most lizard skin products from Brazil, Costa Rica, Ecuador, Peru, Venezuela, India, and Nepal
» Most snakeskin products from Argentina, Brazil, Costa Rica, Ecuador, Guatemala, Mexico, Venezuela, and India

Wild Bird Products
Most wild bird feathers, mounted birds, and skins are prohibited from import to the U.S.

Ivory
Ivory products such as jewelry, figurines, scrimshaw, and piano keys are commonly seen in world markets. Importing ivory whether from African or Asian elephants, whales, walruses, or narwhals is generally prohibited.

Furs
Furs from most large spotted cats such as jaguar, snow leopard, and tiger and from most smaller cats such as ocelot, margay, and tiger cat cannot enter the United States legally. Furs from polar bears and marine mammals such as seals are also prohibited.

Plants
Many plant species are in danger of extinction and are therefore prohibited from import. Generally orchids, cacti, and cycads are not permitted. Remember that even if a plant can be brought into the U.S., all imported plants must undergo an inspection by the Animal and Plant Health Inspection Service and be certified free of disease or pests before importation is allowed.

Coral Reefs

Corals are often fashioned into jewelry and decorative items and sold in enormous quantities. The coral trade has contributed to the destruction of many coral reefs. Therefore, many countries in the Caribbean, the South Pacific, and Southeast Asia prohibit the collection, sale, and export of corals. The U.S. recognizes these restrictions and prohibits their import. To be sure that you can import a coral item, you will have to check with the country where you are purchasing the item to be sure that exportation is allowed.

More and more species are declining in numbers due to exploitation and destruction of their natural habitats. To combat this decline, the U.S. severely restricts the import of products made from wildlife. Despite these restrictions, the U.S. is still the world's largest wildlife consuming country. Maybe we should all give the world's wildlife a break and stop making wildlife product purchases. If you are considering making a purchase of a wildlife product overseas, you need to be sure that you can legally bring it back into the U.S. When in doubt, it is best not to buy. Your souvenir may be confiscated when you reenter the country.

If you are overseas and considering a purchase of a wildlife product, check with the local U.S. Embassy or Consulate. They likely will be able to tell you whether the product you are considering is of local origin and whether its importation into the U.S. is legal. To find out before you go overseas whether a particular wildlife product can be imported into the U.S., contact: the Division of Law Enforcement, U.S. Fish & Wildlife Service, P.O. Box 347, Arlington, Virginia 22203-3247. A private organization also advises about wildlife importing. Contact Traffic USA, World Wildlife Fund, 1250 24th Street NW, Washington, D.C. 20037.

Appendix A

Documents To Take Abroad

- Passport
- Visas (if required)
- Tickets and reservation information
- Cash, traveler's checks, ATM card
- Credit cards
- Traveler's check serial numbers, stored separately
- Credit card numbers
- Credit card and traveler's check companies' phone numbers to report a loss and get replacements
- Frequent Flyer club card
- Telephone calling card
- Driver's license
- International Driving Permit (if you will drive overseas)
- Customs Certificate of Registration (if carrying valuable foreign made items)
- International Certificate of Vaccination (especially for travel to less developed countries)
- Photocopies of important documents. Keep in a separate location.
    - *Passport ID pages (first two pages)
    - *Itinerary
    - *Airline tickets
    - *Driver's license
    - *International Certificate of Vaccination
- Emergency contact. Write contact person's name, address and phone number in the space in your passport.
- Medical card
    - *Name, address, phone number of your physician
    - *Existing medical conditions
    - *Health insurance information including policy number

- Extra passport photos
- Maps and guidebooks
- Some proof of U.S. citizenship, such as an expired passport, a voter's registration card, or a certified copy of your birth certificate. This will help you get a replacement if you lose your passport.
- Addresses and phone numbers of U.S. Embassies and Consulates in the countries you will be visiting.

Consider making and giving copies of things like your passport, itinerary, traveler's check numbers, and airline tickets to someone close to you in the U.S. If you were to lose everything, you could call home, get the needed information and have an easier time replacing the lost items.

Appendix B

U.S. Embassies And Consulates Abroad

NORTH AMERICA

CANADA
Ottawa, Ontario: (Embassy) 100 Wellington Street; Tel: (613) 238-5335.
Calgary, Alberta: (Consulate General) Suite 1050, 615 Macleod Trail SE; Tel: (403) 266-8962.
Halifax, Nova Scotia: (Consulate General) Suite 910, Cogswell Tower, Scotia Square; Tel: (902) 429-2480.
Montreal, Quebec: (Consulate General) 1155 St. Alexander Street; Tel: (514) 398-9695
Quebec, Quebec: (Consulate General) 2 Place Terrasse Dufferin; Tel: (418) 692-2095.
Toronto, Ontario: (Consulate General) 360 University Avenue; Tel: (416) 595-1700.
Vancouver, British Columbia: (Consulate General) 1095 West Pender Street; Tel: (604) 687-6095.

MEXICO
Mexico City: (Embassy) Paseo de la Reforma 305; Tel: [52](5) 211-0042.
Ciudad Juarez: (Consulate General) Avenue Lopez Mateos 924-N; Tel: [52](16) 134-048.
Guadalajara: (Consulate General) Progresso 175; Tel: [52](3) 625-2998.
Hermosillo: (Consulate) Ave. Monterrey 141; Tel: [52](62) 17-2375.
Matamoros: (Consulate) Ave. Primera 2002; Tel: [52](891) 6-7270-2.
Mazatlan: (Consulate) Circunvalacion No. 120 Centro; Tel: [52] (678) 5-2205.
Merida: (Consulate) Paseo Montejo 453; Tel: [52](99) 25-5011.
Monterrey: (Consulate General) Avenida Constitucion 411 Poniente; Tel: [52](83) 45-2120.
Nuevo Laredo: (Consulate) Calle Allende 3330, Col. Jardin; Tel: [52](871) 4-0512.
Tijuana: (Consulate General) Tapachula 96; Tel: [52](66) 81-7400.

The State Department has also set up Resident Consular Agents in ten other locations in Mexico to assist U.S. citizens in serious emergencies.

Acapulco: (Consular Agent) Hotel Club Del Sol; Tel: [52](748) 5-7207, Ext. 273.
Cancun: (Consular Agent) Ave. Coba #30 Esq. Nader; Tel: [52](988) 4-63-99.
Durango: (Consular Agent) Juarez Norte 204; Tel: [52](181) 1-2217.
Mulege: (Consular Agent) Hotel Serenidad; Tel: [52](68) 5-3-0111.
Oaxaca: (Consular Agent) Alcala 201; Tel: [52](951) 6-0654.
Puerto Vallarta: (Consular Agent) Parial del Puerto, Local 12-A; Tel: [52](322) 2-0069.
San Luis Potosi: (Consular Agent) Venustiano Carranza #1430; Tel: [52](481) 7-2501.
San Miguel de Allende: (Consular Agent) Dr. Hernandez Macias #72; Tel: [52](465) 2-2357.
Tampico: (Consular Agent) Ave. Hidalgo #2000, Local 4; Tel: [52] (121) 3-2217.
Vera Cruz: (Consular Agent) Victimas del 25 de Junio #388; Tel: Not available.

SOUTH & CENTRAL AMERICA

ARGENTINA
Buenos Aires: (Embassy) 4300 Columbia, 1425; Tel: [54](1) 777-4533.

BELIZE
Belize City: (Embassy) Gabourel Lane and Hutson Street; Tel: [501](2) 77161.

BOLIVIA
La Paz: (Embassy) Banco Popular Del Peru Bldg. Corner of Calles Mercado and Colon; Tel: [591](2) 350-251.

BRAZIL
Brasilia: (Embassy) Avenida das Nocoes, Lote 3; Tel: [55](61) 321-7272.
Rio de Janeiro: (Consulate General) Avenida Presidente Wilson 147; Tel: [55](21) 292-7117.
Sao Paulo: (Consulate General) Rua Padre Joao Manoel 933; Tel: [55](11) 881-6511.
Porto Alegre: (Consulate) Rua Coronel Genuino 421 (9th fl.); Tel: [55](51) 226-4288.
Recife: (Consulate) Rua Goncalves Maia 163; Tel: [55](81) 221-1412.
Belem: (Consular Agent) Rua Osvaldo Cruz 165; Tel: [55](91) 223-0800.
Fortaleze: (Consular Agent) Instituto Brasil-Estados Undidos, Rua Noguera Acioly 891; Tel: [55](85) 252-1539.
Manaus: (Consular Agent) Rua Recife 1010; Tel: [55](92) 234-4546.
Salvador da Bahia: (Consular Agent) Av. Antonio Carlos Magalhaes, Cidadella Center 1, Suite 410; Tel: [55](71) 358-9166.

CHILE
Santiago: (Embassy) Codina Bldg. 1343 Agustinas; Tel: [56](2) 671-0133.

COLUMBIA
Bogota: (Embassy) Calle 38, No. 8-61; Tel: [57](1) 320-1300.
Barranquilla: (Consulate) Calle 77 Carrera 68, Centro Comercial Mayorista; Tel: [57](58) 457-088.

COSTA RICA
San Jose: (Embassy) Frente al Centro Comercial de Pavas; Tel: (506) 20-39-39.

ECUADOR
Quito: (Embassy) Avenida 12 de Octubre y Avenida Patria; Tel: [593](2) 562-890.
Guayaquil: (Consulate General) 9 de Octubre y Garcia Moreno; Tel: [593](4) 323-570.

EL SALVADOR
San Salvador: (Embassy) Final Blvd., Santa Elena, Station Antiguo Cuscatlan; Tel: (503) 78-4444.

FRENCH GUIANA
Post closed in August 1993.

GUATEMALA
Guatemala City: (Embassy) 7-01 Avenida de la Reforma, Zone 10; Tel: [502](2) 311-541.

GUYANA
Georgetown: (Embassy) 99-100 Young and Duke Sts., Kingston; Tel: [592](2) 54900-9.

HONDURAS
Tegucigalpa: (Embassy) Avenido La Paz; Tel: [504] 36-9320.

NICARAGUA
Managua: (Embassy) Km. 4-1/2 Carretera Sur; Tel: [505](2) 666-010.

PANAMA
Panama City: (Embassy) Balboa Avenue and 38th St. on Panama Bay; Tel: [507] 27-1777.
Cristobal: (Consular Agency) Terminal and Pedro Prestan Sts.; Tel: (507) 41-2440.

PARAGUAY
Asuncion: (Embassy) 1776 Mariscal Lopez Ave; Tel: [595](21) 213-715.

PERU
Lima: (Embassy) Corner Avenidas Inca Garcilaso de la Vega and Espana; Tel: (011-51-14) 33-8000.

SURINAME
Paramaribo: (Embassy) Dr. Sophie Redmondstraat 129; Tel: [597] 472900.

URUGUAY
Montevideo: (Embassy) Lauro Muller 1776; Tel: [598](2) 236-061.

VENEZUELA
Caracas: (Embassy) Avenida Francisco de Miranda and Avenida Principal de la Floresta; Tel: [58](2) 285-2222.
Maracaibo: (Consulate) Edificio Sofimara, Piso 3, Calle 77 Con Avenida 13; Tel: [58](61) 84253.

CARIBBEAN

ANTIGUA & BARBUDA
St. John's: (Embassy) Queen Elizabeth Highway; Tel: (809) 462-3505.

BAHAMAS
Nassau: (Embassy) Mosmar Bldg., Queen Street; Tel: (809) 322-1181.

BARBADOS
Bridgetown: (Embassy) Canadian Imperial Bank of Commerce Building, Broad Street; Tel: (809) 436-4950.

BERMUDA
Hamilton: (Consulate General) Crown Hill, 16 Middle Rd. Devonshire; Tel: (809) 295-1342.

CUBA
Havana: (U.S. Interests Section) Swiss Embassy, Calzada between L and M, Vedado; Tel: 33-3551/9.

DOMINICAN REPUBLIC
Santo Domingo: (Embassy) Calle Cesar Nicolas Penson & Calle Leopoldo Navarro; Tel: (809) 541-2171.
Puerto Plata: (Consular Agent) 51 Beller Street; Tel: (809) 586-4204.

GRENADA
St. George's: (Embassy) Port Salines; Tel: (809) 44-1173.

HAITI
Port-au-Prince: (Embassy) Harry Truman Blvd. Tel: [509] 22-0354.

JAMAICA
Kingston: (Embassy) Jamaica Mutual Life Center, 2 Oxford Road, 3rd Fl.; Tel: (809) 929-4850.

Montego Bay: (Consular Agent) St. James Place, Second Floor, Glocester Avenue; Tel: (809) 952-0160.

NETHERLANDS ANTILLES
Curacao: (Consulate General) St. Anna Boulevard 19; Tel: [599](9) 61-3066.

TRINIDAD & TOBAGO
Port of Spain: (Embassy) 15 Queen's Park West; Tel: (809) 622-6372.

WESTERN EUROPE

AUSTRIA
Vienna: (Embassy) Boltzmanngasse 16; Tel: [43](1) 313-39.
Salzburg: Post closed September 1993.

BELGIUM
Brussels: (Embassy) 27 Boulevard du Regent; Tel: [32](2) 513-3830.

DENMARK
Copenhagen: (Embassy) Dag Hammarskjolds Alle 24; Tel: [45](31) 42-31-44.

FINLAND
Helsinki: (Embassy) Itainen Puistotie 14A; Tel: [358](0) 171931.

FRANCE
Paris: (Embassy) 2 Avenue Gabriel; Tel: [33](1) 4296-12-02.
Bordeaux: (Consulate General) 22 Cours du Marechal Foch; Tel: [33](56) 52-65-95.
Marseille: (Consulate General) 12 Boulevard Paul Peytral; Tel: [33](91) 549-200.
Strasbourg: (Consulate General) 15 Ave. D'Alsace; Tel: [33](88) 24-06-95.
Nice: (Consular Agent) 31 Rue du Marechal Joffre; Tel: [33](93) 88-8955.

GERMANY
Bonn: (Embassy) Deichmanns Aue 29; Tel: [49](228) 3391.
Berlin: (Embassy Branch Office) Neustaedtische Kirchstrasse 4-5; Tel: [49](30) 238-5174.
Frankfurt: (Consulate General) Siesmayerstrasse 21; Tel: [49](69) 7535-0.
Hamburg: (Consulate General) Alsterufer 27/28; Tel: [49](40) 411710.
Leipzig: (Consulate General) Wilhelm Seyfferth Strasse 4; Tel: [49](341) 211-78-66.
Munich: (Consulate General) Koeniginstrasse 5; Tel: [49](89) 28880.
Stuttgart: (Consulate General) Urbanstrasse 7; Tel: [49](711) 21008-0.

GREECE
Athens: (Embassy) 91 Vasilissis Sophias Blvd.; Tel: [30](1) 721-2951.
Thessaloniki: (Consulate General) 59 Leoforos Nikis; Tel: [30](31) 242905.

ICELAND
Reykjavik: (Embassy) Laufasvegur 21; Tel: [354](1) 629100.

IRELAND
Dublin: (Embassy) 42 Elgin Rd., Ballsbridge; Tel: [353](1) 668-7122.

ITALY
Rome: (Embassy) Via Veneto 119/A; Tel: [39](6) 46741.
Florence: (Consulate General) Lungarno Amerigo Vespucci 38; Tel: [39](55) 239-8276.
Genoa: Post closed June 1993.
Milan: (Consulate General) Via Principe Amedeo, 2/10; Tel: [39](2) 290-351.
Naples: (Consulate General) Piazza della Repubblica; Tel: [39](81) 761-4303.
Palermo: (Consulate General) Via Vaccarini 1; Tel: [39](91) 343-532.

LUXEMBOURG
Luxembourg: (Embassy) 22 Blvd. Emmanuel-Servais; Tel: [352] 460123.

MALTA
Valletta: (Embassy) Development House, 2nd Fl., St. Anne Street, Floriana; Tel: [356] 235960.

NETHERLANDS
The Hague: (Embassy) Lange Voorhout 102; Tel: [31](70) 310-9209.
Amsterdam: (Consulate General) Museumplein 19; Tel: [31](20) 5755 309.

NORWAY
Oslo: (Embassy) Drammensveien 18; Tel: [47] 22-44-85-50.

PORTUGAL
Lisbon: (Embassy) Avenida das Forcas Armadas; Tel: [351](1) 726-6600.
Ponta Delgada, Sao Miguel, Azores: (Consulate) Avenida D. Henrique; Tel: [351](96) 22216.
Funchal, Madeira: (Consular Agency) Avenida Luisde Camoes; Tel: [351](91) 743-429.

SPAIN
Madrid: (Embassy) Serrano 75; Tel: [34](1) 577-4000.
Barcelona: (Consulate General) Reina Elisenda 23; Tel: [34](3) 280-2227.
Bilboa: (Consulate) Lehendakari Agirre 11-3; Tel: [34](4) 475-8300.

SWEDEN
Stockholm: (Embassy) Strandvagen 101; Tel: [46](8) 783-5300.

SWITZERLAND
Bern: (Embassy) Jubilaeumstrasse 93; Tel: [41](31) 357-7011.
Geneva: Post closed July 1993.
Zurich: (Consulate General) Zollikerstrasse 141; Tel: [41](1) 422-25-66.

U.S. Embassies & Consulates Abroad 147

UNITED KINGDOM
London, England: (Embassy) 24/31 Grosvenor Square; Tel: [44](71) 499-9000.
Belfast, Northern Ireland: (Consulate General) Queen's House, 14 Queen St.; Tel: [44](232) 328239.
Edinburgh, Scotland: (Consulate General) 3 Regent Terrace.; Tel: [44](31) 556-8315.

THE VATICAN
Vatican City: (Embassy) Villino Pacelli, Via Aurelia 294; Tel: [396] 46741.

EASTERN EUROPE

ALBANIA
Tirane: (Embassy) Tirana Rruga E. Elbansanit 103; Tel: 355-42-32875.

BOSNIA-HERZEGOVINA
Sarajevo: (Embassy) Djure Djakovica 43; Tel: [387](71) 659-992.

BULGARIA
Sofia: (Embassy) 1 Saborna St.; Tel: [359](2) 88-48-01.

CROATIA
Zagreb: (Embassy) Andrije Hebranga 2; Tel: [38](41) 444-800.

CZECH REPUBLIC
Prague: (Embassy) Trziste 15; Tel: [42](2) 536-641.

HUNGARY
Budapest: (Embassy) V. Szabadsag Ter 12; Tel: [36](1) 112-6450.

POLAND
Warsaw: (Embassy) Aleje Ujazdowskie 29/31; Tel: [48](2) 628-3041.
Krakow: (Consulate General) Ulica Stolarska 9; Tel: [48](12) 229764.
Poznan: (Consulate General) Ulica Chopina 4; Tel: [48](61) 551088.

ROMANIA
Bucharest: (Embassy) Strada Tudor Arghezi 7-9; Tel: [40](1) 312-0149.

SERBIA-MONTENEGRO
Belgrade: (Embassy) Kneza Milosa 50; Tel: [381](11) 645-655.

SLOVAK REPUBLIC
Bratislava: (Embassy) Hviezdoslavovo Namestie 4; Tel: [42](7) 330861.

SLOVENIA
Ljubljana: (Embassy) Prazakova 4; Tel: [386](61) 301-427.

RUSSIA & FORMER SOVIET UNION

ARMENIA
Yerevan: (Embassy) 18 General Bagramian St. Tel: (7-8852) 151-144.

AZERBAIJAN
Baku: (Embassy) Prospect Azadlig 83; Tel: (7-8922) 96-00-19.

BELARUS
Minsk: (Embassy) Starovilenskaya Ulitsa 46; Tel: (7-0172) 34-65-37.

ESTONIA
Tallinn: (Embassy) Kentmanni 20; Tel: [372](6) 312-021.

GEORGIA
Tbilisi: (Embassy) 25 Antonely Street; Tel: (7-8832) 989-967.

KAZAKHSTAN
Almaty: (Embassy) 99/97 Furmanova St.; Tel: (7-3272) 63-34-05.

KYRGYZSTAN
Bishkek: (Embassy) Erkindik Prospekt #66; Tel: (7-3312) 22-29-20.

LATVIA
Riga: (Embassy) Raina Boulevard 7; Tel: 46-9-882-0046.

LITHUANIA
Vilnius: (Embassy) Akmenu 6; Tel: 370-2-223-031.

MOLDOVA
Chisinau: (Embassy) 103 Strada Alexi Mateevici; Tel: [373](2) 23-37-72.

RUSSIA
Moscow: (Embassy) Novinskiy Bulvar 19/23; Tel: [7](095) 252-2451.
St. Petersburg: (Consulate General) Furshtadskaya Ulitsa 15; Tel: [7](812) 275-1701.
Vladivostok: (Consulate General) Ulitsa Mordovtseva 12; Tel: [7](4232) 268-458.

TAJIKISTAN
Dushanbe: (Embassy) Hotel Independence, 105A Rudaki Prospect; Tel: [7](3772) 248-233.

TURKMENISTAN
Ashgabat: (Embassy) Yubilenaya Hotel; Tel: [7] 36320 24-49-25.

UKRAINE
Kiev: (Embassy) 10 Yuria Kotsyubinskovo; Tel: [7](044) 244-7349.

UZBEKISTAN
Tashkent: (Embassy) 82 Chelanzanskaya; Tel: [7](3712)77-14-07.

MIDDLE EAST & NORTH AFRICA

ALGERIA
Algiers: (Embassy) 4 Chemin Cheich Bachir El-Ibrahimi; Tel: [213](2) 601-425/255/186.
Oran: Post closed June 1993.

BAHRAIN
Manama: (Embassy) Building 979, Road No. 3119, Zinj District (Next to Al Ahli Sports Club); Tel: (973) 273-300.

CYPRUS
Nicosia: (Embassy) Metochiou and Ploutarchou Streets, Engomi; Tel: [357](2) 476100.

EGYPT
Cairo: (Embassy) 8 Kamal El-Din Salah Street, Garden City; Tel: [20](2) 355-7371.
Alexandria: Post closed September 1993.

IRAN
Tehran: (U.S. Interests Section) Embassy of Switzerland, Bucharest & 17th Street, No. 5; Tel: [98](21) 625-223.

IRAQ
Baghdad: U.S. diplomatic operations suspended.

ISRAEL
Tel Aviv: (Embassy) 71 Hayarkon Street; Tel: [972](3) 517-4338.
Haifa: (Consular Agency, limited services) 12 Jerusalem Street; Tel: [972](4) 670-615.
Jerusalem: (Consulate General) 18 Agron Road; Tel: [972](2) 253-288.

JORDAN
Amman: (Embassy) Abdoun; Tel: [962](6) 820-101.

KUWAIT
Kuwait City: (Embassy) Gulf Road (Near Kuwait International Hotel); Tel: [965] 242-4151.

LEBANON
Beirut: (Embassy) Antelias; Tel: [961](1) 402-200.

LIBYA
Tripoli: (U.S. Interests Section) Embassy of Belgium, Tower 4, That al Imad Complex; Tel: [218](21) 33771.

MOROCCO
Rabat: (Embassy) 2 Avenue de Marrakech; Tel: [212](7) 762-265.
Casablanca: (Consulate General) 8 Boulevard Moulay Youssef; Tel: [212](2) 264-550.

OMAN
Muscat: (Embassy) Madinat Qaboos; Tel: [968] 698-989.

QATAR
Doha: (Embassy) 149 Ali Bin Ahmed St., Farig Bin Omran (opposite TV station); Tel: [974] 864-701.

SAUDI ARABIA
Riyadh: (Embassy) Collector Road M, Riyadh Diplomatic Quarter; Tel: [966](1) 488-3800.
Dhahran: (Consulate General) Between Aramco Headquarters and Dhahran Int'l Airport; Tel: [966](3) 891-3200.
Jeddah: (Consulate General) Palestine Road, Ruwais; Tel: [966](2) 667-0080.

SYRIA
Damascus: (Embassy) Abu Roumaneh, Al-Mansur Street No. 2; Tel: [963](11) 333-814.

TUNISIA
Tunis: (Embassy) 144 Ave. de la Liberte; Tel: [216](1) 782-566.

TURKEY
Ankara: (Embassy) 110 Ataturk Blvd.; Tel: [90](312) 468-6110.
Adana: (Consulate) Ataturk Caddesi; Tel: [90](322) 453-9106.
Istanbul: (Consulate General) 104-108 Mesrutiyet Caddesi, Tepebasi; Tel: [90](212) 251-3602.
Izmir: Post closed June 1993.

UNITED ARAB EMIRATES
Abu Dhabi: (Embassy) Al-Sudan St.; Tel: [971](2) 436-691.
Dubai: (Consulate General) Dubai International Trade Center, 21st Floor; Tel: [971](4) 313-115.

YEMEN
Sanaa: (Embassy) Dhar Himyar Zone, Sheraton Hotel District; Tel: [967](1) 238-843.

SUB-SAHARAN AFRICA

ANGOLA
Luanda: (Embassy) Rua Major Kanyangunla No. 132/136; Tel: [244](2) 39-69-27.

BENIN
Cotonou: (Embassy) Rue Caporal Bernard Anani; Tel: [229] 300-650.

BOTSWANA
Gaborone: (Embassy) Embassy Drive, Government Enclave; Tel: [267] 353-982.

BURKINA FASO
Ouagadougou: (Embassy) Avenue Raoul Follerau; Tel: [226] 306-723.

BURUNDI
Bujumbura: (Embassy) 1720 Avenue des Etats-Unis; Tel: [257] (2) 23454.

CAMEROON
Yaounde: (Embassy) Rue Nachtigal; Tel: [237] 234-014.

CAPE VERDE
Praia: (Embassy) Rua Abilio Macedo 81; Tel: [238] 61-56-16.

CENTRAL AFRICAN REPUBLIC
Bangui: (Embassy) Avenue David Dacko; Tel: [236] 610-200.

CHAD
N'Djamena: (Embassy) Avenue Felix Eboue; Tel: [235] 516-218.

COMOROS
Moroni: Post closed September 1993.

CONGO
Brazzaville: (Embassy) Avenue Amilcar Cabral; Tel: (242) 832-070.

COTE D'IVOIRE
Abidjan: (Embassy) 5 Rue Jesse Owens; Tel: (225) 21-09-79.

DJIBOUTI
Djibouti: (Embassy) Plateau de Serpent, Blvd. Marechal Joffre; Tel: [253] 353-995.

EQUATORIAL GUINEA
Malabo: (Embassy) Calle de Los Ministros; Tel: [250] (9) 2185.

ERITREA
Asmara: (Embassy) 34 Zera Yacob St.; Tel: [291] (1) 123-720.

ETHIOPIA
Addis Ababa: (Embassy) Entoto St.; Tel: [251] (1) 550-666.

GABON
Libreville: (Embassy) Blvd. de la Mer; Tel: [241] 762-003.

GAMBIA
Banjul: (Embassy) Fajara (East), Kasiraba Ave; Tel: (220) 92-856.

GHANA
Accra: (Embassy) Ring Road East; Tel: [233] (21) 775348.

GUINEA
Conakry: (Embassy) 2nd Blvd. and 9th Ave.; Tel: (224) 44-15-20.

GUINEA-BISSAU
Bissau: (Embassy) Avenida Domingos Ramos, 1067 Bissau Codex; Tel: [245] 20-1139.

KENYA
Nairobi: (Embassy) Moi/Haile Selassie Ave.; Tel: [254] (2) 334-141.
Mombasa: Post closed May 1993.

LESOTHO
Maseru: (Embassy) Maseru 100; Tel: [266] 312-666.

LIBERIA
Monrovia: (Embassy) 111 United Nations Drive, Mamba Point; Tel: [231] 222-991.

MADAGASCAR
Antananarivo: (Embassy) 14-16 Rue Rainitovo, Antsahavola; Tel: [261](2) 21257.

MALAWI
Lilongwe: (Embassy) Lilongwe 3; Tel: [265] 783-166.

MALI
Bamako: (Embassy) Rue Rochester NY and Rue Mohamed V; Tel: [223] 225470.

MAURITANIA
Nouakchott: Between Presidency Building and Spanish Embassy; Tel: [222](2) 52660.

MAURITIUS
Port Louis: (Embassy) Rogers House, 4th Floor, John Kennedy Street; Tel: [230] 208-9763.

MOZAMBIQUE
Maputo: (Embassy) Avenida Kenneth Kaunda 193; Tel: [258](1) 49-27-97.

NAMIBIA
Windhoek: (Embassy) Ausplan Building, 14 Lossen St.; Tel: [264](61) 221-601.

NIGER
Niamey: (Embassy) Rue Des Ambassades; Tel: [227] 72-26-61.

NIGERIA
Lagos: (Embassy) 2 Eleke Crescent; Tel: [234](1) 261-0097.
Kaduna: (Consulate General) 9 Maska Rd.; Tel: [234](62) 235990.

RWANDA
Kigali: (Embassy) Blvd. de la Revolution; Tel: [250] 75601.

SENEGAL
Dakar: (Embassy) Avenue Jean XXIII; Tel: [221] 23-42-96.

SEYCHELLES
Victoria: (Embassy) Victoria House; Tel: [248] 225256.

SIERRA LEONE
Freetown: (Embassy) Corner Walpole and Siaka Stevens St.; Tel: [232](22) 226-481.

SOMALIA
Mogadishu: Post evacuated January 1991.

SOUTH AFRICA
Pretoria: (Embassy) 877 Pretorius St.; Tel: [27](12) 342-1048.
Cape Town: (Consulate General) Broadway Industries Center, Heerengracht, Foreshore; Tel: [27](21) 214-280.
Durban: (Consulate General) Durban Bay House, 29th Fl., 333 Smith St.; Tel: [27](31) 304-4737.
Johannesburg: (Consulate General) Kine Center, 11th Fl., Commissioner and Krulis Sts.; Tel: [27](11) 331-1681.

SUDAN
Khartoum: (Embassy) Sharia Ali Abdul Latif; Tel: 74700.

SWAZILAND
Mbabane: (Embassy) Central Bank Bldg., Warner Street; Tel: [268] 46441.

TANZANIA
Dar Es Salaam: (Embassy) 36 Laibon Rd. (Off Bagamoyo Rd.); Tel: [255](51) 66010.

TOGO
Lome: (Embassy) Rue Pelletier Caventou & Rue Vauban; Tel: [228] 21-77-17.

UGANDA
Kampala: (Embassy) Parliament Ave.; Tel: [256](41) 259792.

ZAIRE
Kinshasa: (Embassy) 310 Avenue des Aviateurs; Tel: [243](12) 21532.
Lubumbashi: (Consulate General) 1029 Blvd. Kamanyola; Tel: [243](11) 222324.

ZAMBIA
Lusaka: (Embassy) Corner of Independence and United Nations Aves.; Tel: [260](1) 228-595.

ZIMBABWE
Harare: (Embassy) 172 Herbert Chitepo Ave.; Tel: [263](4) 794-521.

ASIA

AFGHANISTAN
Kabul: Embassy evacuated January 1989.

BANGLADESH
Dhaka: (Embassy) Diplomatic Enclave, Madani Ave., Baridhara; Tel: [880](2) 884700.

BHUTAN
None: Contact U.S. diplomatic posts in India or Bangladesh for assistance.

BRUNEI
Bandar Seri Begawan: (Embassy) Third Floor, Teck Guan Plaza; Tel: [673](2) 229-670.

BURMA
Rangoon: (Embassy) 581 Merchant St.; Tel: [95](1) 82055.

CAMBODIA
Phnom Penh: (Embassy) 27 EO Street; Tel: (855) 23-26436.

CHINA
Beijing: (Embassy) Xiu Shui Bei Jie 3; Tel: [86](1) 532-3831.
Guangzhou (Consulate General) No. 1 South Shamian Street, Shamian Island; Tel: [86](20) 888-8911.
Shanghai: (Consulate General) 1469 Huai Hai Middle Road; Tel: [86](21) 433-6880.

U.S. Embassies & Consulates Abroad 155

Shenyang: (Consulate General) 52, 14th Wei Road, Heping District; Tel: [86](24) 282-0000.
Chengdu: (Consulate General) Renmin Nan Lu-Duan 4, Lingshiquan Lu; Tel: [86](28) 582-222.

HONG KONG
Hong Kong: (Embassy) 26 Garden Rd.; Tel: [852] 523-9011.

INDIA
New Delhi: (Embassy) Shanti Path, Chanakyapuri; Tel: [91](11) 600651.
Bombay: (Consulate General) Lincoln House, 78 Bhulabhai Desai Rd.; Tel: [91](22) 363-3611.
Calcutta: (Consulate General) 5/1 Ho Chi Minh Sarani; Tel: [91](33) 242-3611.
Madras: (Consulate General) 220 Mount Rd.; Tel: [91](44) 825-0240.

INDONESIA
Jakarta: (Embassy) Medan Merdeka Selatan 5; Tel: [62](21) 360-360.
Medan: (Consulate General) Jalan Imam Bonjol 13; Tel: [62](61) 322200.
Surabaya: (Consulate General) Jalan Raya Dr. Sutomo 33; Tel: [62](31) 582287.

JAPAN
Tokyo: (Embassy) 10-5, Akasaka 1-chome, Minato-ku (107); Tel: [81](3) 3224-5000.
Naha, Okinawa: (Consulate General) 2564 Nishihara, Urasoe City; Tel: [81](98) 876-4243.
Osaka-Kobe: (Consulate General) 11-5, Nishitenma 2-chome, Kita-ku; Tel: [81](6) 315-5900.
Sapporo: (Consulate General) Kita 1-Jo Nishi 28-chome, Chou-ku; Tel: [81](11) 641-1115.
Fukuoka: (Consulate) 5-26 Ohori 2-chome, Chuo-ku; Tel: [81](92) 751-9331.
Nagoya: (Consulate) Nishiki SIS Building 6F 10-33 Nishiki 3-chome Naka-ku; Tel: [81](52) 203-4011.

KOREA (South)
Seoul: (Embassy) 82 Sejong-Ro, Chongro-ku; Tel: [82](2) 397-4114.
Pusan: (Consulate) 24 2-Ka, Daechung-Dong, Chung-ku; Tel: [82](51) 246-7791.

LAOS
Vientiane: (Embassy) Rue Bartholonie; Tel: [856] 2220.

MALAYSIA
Kuala Lumpur: (Embassy) 376 Jalan Tun Razak; Tel: [60](3) 248-9011.

MALDIVES
Male: (Consular Agent) Mandhu Edurruge, 20-05 Violet Magu; Tel: 322581.

MONGOLIA
Ulaanbaatar: (Embassy) Big Ring Road; Tel: [976](1) 329095.

NEPAL
Kathmandu: (Embassy) Pani Pokhari; Tel: [977](1) 411179.

PAKISTAN
Islamabad: (Embassy) Diplomatic Enclave, Ramna 5; Tel: [92] (51) 826161.
Karachi: (Consulate General) 8 Abdullah Haroon Rd; Tel: [92](21) 568170.
Lahore: (Consulate General) 50 Sharah-E-Bin Badees (50 Empress Rd.); Tel: [92](42) 636-5530.
Peshawar: (Consulate) 11 Hospital Road, Peshawar Cantt; Tel: [92](521) 279801.

PHILIPPINES
Manila: (Embassy) 1201 Roxas Blvd.; Tel: (632) 521-7116.
Cebu: (Consulate) 3rd Fl., PCI Bank Building, Gorordo Ave.; Tel: [63](32) 311-261.

SINGAPORE
Singapore: (Embassy) 30 Hill St.; Tel: (65) 338-0251.

SRI LANKA
Colombo: (Embassy) 210 Galle Rd.; Tel: [94](1) 448007.

TAIWAN
There is no State Department presence in Taiwan. Contact an office of the American Institute in Taiwan at the following locations if assistance is needed while visiting Taiwan.
Taipei: #7 Lane 134, Hsin Yi Road, Section 3; Tel: [886](2) 709-2000.
Kaohsiung: 5th Fl., #2 Chung Cheng 3rd Road; Tel: [886](7) 224-0154.

THAILAND
Bangkok: (Embassy) 95 Wireless Rd.; Tel: [66](2) 252-5040.
Chiang Mai: (Consulate General) Vidhayanond Rd.; Tel: [66](53) 252-629.
Songkhla: Post closed June 1993.
Udorn: (Consulate) 35/6 Supakitjanya Rd.; Tel: [66](42) 244-273.

VIETNAM
At press time, the U.S. and Vietnam were in the process of establishing diplomatic posts in each other's countries.

PACIFIC

AUSTRALIA
Canberra: (Embassy) Moonah Place; Tel: [61](6) 270-5000.
Melbourne: (Consulate General) 553 St. Kilda Road; Tel: [61](3) 526-5900.

Sydney: (Consulate General) MLC Centre, 59th Fl., 19-29 Martin Place; Tel: [61](2) 373-9200.
Perth: (Consulate General) 16 St. Georges Terrace, 13th Fl.; Tel: [61](9) 231-9400.
Brisbane: (Consulate) 383 Wickham Terrace, 4th Fl.; Tel: [61](7) 405-5555.

FIJI
Suva: (Embassy) 31 Loftus St.; Tel: [679] 314-466.

MARSHALL ISLANDS
Majuro: (Embassy) Near Morman Church and "Blue Wall" compound; Tel: (692) 247-4011.

MICRONESIA
Kolonia: (Embassy) Lower Pics area across from Agricultural Station; Tel: [691] 320-2187.

NEW ZEALAND
Wellington: (Embassy) 29 Fitzherbert Terrace, Thorndon; Tel: [64](4) 472-2068.
Auckland: (Consulate General) Yorkshire General Bldg. 4th Fl., Corner of Shortland & O'Connell Sts.; Tel: [64](9) 303-2724.

PALAU
Koror: (U.S. Liaison Office); Tel: (680) 488-2920.

PAPUA NEW GUINEA
Port Moresby: (Embassy) Armit Street; Tel: (675) 211-455.

SOLOMON ISLANDS
Honiara: Post closed July 1993.

WESTERN SAMOA
Apia: (Embassy) John Williams Building, 5th Fl., Beach Road; Tel: (685) 21-631.

Appendix C

Foreign Embassies In The U.S.

NORTH AMERICA

Embassy of Canada
501 Pennsylvania Ave. NW
Washington, D.C. 20001
(202) 682-1740

Embassy of Mexico
1911 Pennsylvania Ave. NW
Washington, D.C. 20006
(202) 728-1600

SOUTH & CENTRAL AMERICA

Embassy of Argentina
1600 New Hampshire Ave. NW
Washington, D.C. 20009
(202) 939-6400

Embassy of Belize
2535 Massachusetts Ave. NW
Washington, D.C. 20008
(202) 332-9636

Embassy of Bolivia
3014 Massachusetts Ave. NW
Washington, D.C. 20008
(202) 483-4410

Embassy of Brazil
3006 Massachusetts Ave. NW
Washington, D.C. 20008
(202) 745-2700

Embassy of Chile
1732 Massachusetts Ave. NW
Washington, D.C. 20036
(202) 785-1746

Embassy of Columbia
2118 Leroy Place NW
Washington, D.C. 20008
(202) 387-8338

Embassy of Costa Rica
2114 S Street NW
Washington, D.C. 20008
(202) 234-2945

Embassy of Ecuador
2535 15th St. NW
Washington, D.C. 20009
(202) 234-7200

Embassy of El Salvador
2308 California St. NW
Washington, D.C. 20008
(202) 265-9671

Galapagos Islands–Contact
Embassy of Ecuador

Embassy of Guatemala
2220 R Street NW
Washington, D.C. 20008
(202) 745-4952

Embassy of Guyana
2490 Tracy Place NW
Washington, D.C. 20008
(202) 265-6900

French Guiana–Contact
Embassy of France

Embassy of Honduras
3007 Tilden St. NW
Washington, D.C. 20008
(202) 966-7702

Embassy of Nicaragua
1627 New Hampshire Ave. NW
Washington, D.C. 20009
(202) 939-6570

Embassy of Panama
2862 McGill Terrace NW
Washington, D.C. 20008
(202) 483-1407

Embassy of Paraguay
2400 Massachusetts Ave. NW
Washington, D.C. 20008
(202) 483-6960

Embassy of Peru
1700 Massachusetts Ave. NW
Washington, D.C. 20036
(202) 833-9860

Embassy of Suriname
4301 Connecticut Ave. NW
Suite 108
Washington, D.C. 20008
(202) 244-7488

Embassy of Uruguay
1918 F Street NW
Washington, D.C. 20006
(202) 331-1313

Embassy of Venezuela
1099 30th St. NW
Washington, D.C. 20007
(202) 342-2214

CARIBBEAN

Embassy of Antigua & Barbuda
3400 International Dr. NW
Suite 4M
Washington, D.C. 20008
(202) 362-5122

Aruba–Contact Embassy of
the Netherlands

Embassy of the Bahamas
2220 Massachusetts Ave. NW
Washington, D.C. 20008
(202) 319-2660

Embassy of Barbados
2144 Wyoming Ave. NW
Washington, D.C. 20008
(202) 939-9200

Bermuda–Contact
Embassy of United Kingdom

British Virgin Islands–Contact
Embassy of United Kingdom

Cayman Islands–Contact Embassy
of United Kingdom

Cuban Interests Section
2639 16th Street NW
Washington, D.C. 20009
(202) 797-8518

Dominica–Contact Embassy of
Barbados

Embassy of Dominican Republic
1715 22nd Street NW
Washington, D.C. 20008
(202) 332-6280

Embassy of Grenada
1701 New Hampshire Ave. NW
Washington, D.C. 20009
(202) 265-2561

Guadeloupe–Contact Embassy
of France

Embassy of Haiti
2311 Massachusetts Ave. NW
Washington, D.C. 20008
(202) 332-4090

Embassy of Jamaica
1850 K St. NW, Suite 355
Washington, D.C. 20006
(202) 452-0660

Martinique–Contact
Embassy of France

Montserrat–Contact Embassy
of United Kingdom

Netherland Antilles–Contact
Embassy of the Netherlands

Embassy of St. Kitts & Nevis
2100 M St. NW, Suite 608
Washington, D.C. 20037
(202) 833-3550

Embassy of St. Lucia
2100 M St. NW, Suite 309
Washington, D.C. 20037
(202) 463-7378

St. Martin–Contact Embassy of France

Embassy of St. Vincent &
the Grenadines
1717 Massachusetts Ave. NW, # 102
Washington, D.C. 20036
(202) 462-7806

Embassy of Trinidad & Tobago
1708 Massachusetts Ave. NW
Washington, D.C. 20036
(202) 467-6490

Turks & Caicos–Contact Embassy
of the United Kingdom

West Indies, British–Contact
Embassy of United Kingdom

West Indies, French–Contact
Embassy of France

WESTERN EUROPE

Andorra–Contact Embassy of France

Embassy of Austria
3524 International Court NW
Washington, D.C. 20008
(202) 895-6700

Embassy of Belgium
3330 Garfield St. NW
Washington, D.C. 20008
(202) 333-6900

Embassy of Denmark
3200 Whitehave St. NW
Washington, D.C. 20008
(202) 234-4300

Embassy of Finland
3216 New Mexico Ave. NW
Washington, D.C. 30016
(202) 363-2430

Foreign Embassies In The U.S.

Embassy of France
4101 Reservoir Rd. NW
Washington, D.C. 20007
(202) 944-6000

Embassy of Germany
4645 Reservoir Rd. NW
Washington, D.C. 20007
(202) 298-4000

Gibraltar–Contact Embassy
of United Kingdom

Embassy of Greece
2221 Massachusetts Ave. NW
Washington, D.C. 20008
(202) 939-5800

Embassy of Iceland
2022 Connecticut Ave. NW
Washington, D.C. 20008
(202) 265-6653

Embassy of Ireland
2234 Massachusetts Ave. NW
Washington, D.C. 20008
(202) 462-3939

Embassy of Italy
1601 Fuller St. NW
Washington, D.C. 20009
(202) 328-5500

Embassy of Luxembourg
2200 Massachusetts Ave. NW
Washington, D.C. 20008
(202) 265-4171

Embassy of Malta
2017 Connecticut Ave. NW
Washington, D.C. 20008
(202) 462-3611

Embassy of the Netherlands
4200 Linnean Ave. NW
Washington, D.C. 20008
(202) 244-5300

Embassy of Norway
2720 34th Street NW
Washington, D.C. 20008
(202) 333-6000

Embassy of Portugal
2125 Kalorama Rd. NW
Washington, D.C. 20008
(202) 328 8610

Consulate of San Marino
1155 21st St. NW, Suite 400
Washington, D.C. 20036
(202) 223-3517

Embassy of Spain
2375 Pennsylvania Ave. NW
Washington, D.C. 20009
(202) 728-2330

Embassy of Sweden
600 New Hampshire Ave. NW
Suites 1200 & 715
Washington, D.C. 20037
(202) 944-5600

Embassy of Switzerland
2900 Cathedral Ave. NW
Washington, D.C. 20008
(202) 745-7900

Embassy of the United Kingdom
(England, N. Ireland, Scotland, Wales)
3100 Massachusetts Ave. NW
Washington, D.C. 20008
(202) 462-1340

Embassy of the Vatican
3339 Massachusetts Ave. NW
Washington, D.C. 20008
(202) 333-7121

EASTERN EUROPE

Embassy of Albania
1150 18th St. NW
Washington, D.C. 20036
(202) 223-4942

Embassy of Bulgaria
1621 22nd Street NW
Washington, D.C. 20008
(202) 387-7969

Embassy of Croatia
2343 Massachusetts Ave. NW
Washington, D.C. 20008
(202) 588-5899

Embassy of Czech Republic
3900 Spring of Freedom St.
Washington, D.C. 20008
(202) 363-6315

Embassy of Hungary
3910 Shoemaker St. NW
Washington, D.C. 20008
(202) 362-6730

Embassy of Poland
2640 16th Street NW
Washington, D.C. 20009
(202) 234-3800

Embassy of Romania
1607 23rd Street NW
Washington, D.C. 20008
(202) 332-4846

Offices of Serbia & Montenegro
2410 California St. NW
Washington, D.C. 20008
(202) 462-6566

Embassy of Slovak Republic
2201 Wisconsin Ave. NW
Washington, D.C. 20007
(202) 363-6315

Embassy of Slovenia
1300 19th St. NW, Suite 410
Washington, D.C. 20036
(202) 828-1650

RUSSIA & FORMER SOVIET UNION

Embassy of Armenia
122 C St. NW, Suite 360
Washington, D.C. 20001
(202) 628-5766

Embassy of Azerbaijan
927 15th St. NW, Suite 700
Washington, D.C. 20005
(202) 842-0001

Embassy of Belarus
1619 New Hampshire Ave. NW
Washington, D.C. 20009
(202) 986-1604

Embassy of Estonia
103015th St. Suite 1000
Washington, D.C. 20005
(202) 789-0320

Georgia–Contact Embassy of Russia

Embassy of Kazkakhstan
3421 Massachusetts Ave. NW
Washington, D.C. 20008
(202) 333-4504

Embassy of Kyrgyzstan
1511 K St. NW, Suite 705
Washington, D.C. 20005
(202) 347-3732

Embassy of Latvia
4325 17th Street NW
Washington, D.C. 20011
(202) 726-8213

Embassy of Lithuania
2622 16th St. NW
Washington, D.C. 20008
(202) 234-5860

Moldova–Contact Embassy
of Russia

Embassy of Russia
1125 16th Street NW
Washington, D.C. 20036
(202) 628-7551

Tajikistan–Contact Embassy
of Russia

Turkmenistan–Contact
Embassy of Russia

Embassy of Ukraine
3350 M Street NW
Washington, D.C. 20007
(202) 333-0606

Embassy of Uzbekistan
2000 Pennsylvania Ave. NW,
Suite 6500
Washington, D.C. 20006
(202) 778-0107

MIDDLE EAST & NORTHERN AFRICA

Embassy of Algeria
2118 Kalorama Rd., NW
Washington, D.C. 20008
(202) 265-2800

Embassy of Bahrain
3502 International Dr. NW
Washington, D.C. 20008
(202) 342-0741

Embassy of Cyprus
2211 R Street NW
Washington, D.C. 20008
(202) 462-5772

Embassy of Egypt
2310 Decatur Place NW
Washington, D.C. 20008
(202) 232-5400

Iranian Interests Section
Contact Embassy of Pakistan
2209 Wisconsin Ave. NW
Washington, D.C. 20007
(202) 965-4990

Iraqi Interests Section
Contact Embassy of Algeria
1801 P Street NW
Washington, D.C. 20036
(202) 483-7500

Embassy of Israel
3514 International Dr. NW
Washington, D.C. 20008
(202) 364-5500

Embassy of Jordan
3504 International Dr. NW
Washington, D.C. 20008
(202) 966-2664

Embassy of Kuwait
2940 Tilden St. NW
Washington, D.C. 20008
(202) 966-0702

Embassy of Lebanon
2560 28th St. NW
Washington, D.C. 20008
(202) 939-6300

Libya–Contact
Office of Foreign Assets Control
Department of Treasury
1331 G Street NW
Washington, D.C. 20220

Embassy of Morocco
1601 21st Street NW
Washington, D.C. 20009
(202) 462-7979

Embassy of Oman
2342 Massachusetts Ave. NW
Washington, D.C. 20008
(202) 387-1980

Embassy of Qatar
600 New Hampshire Ave. NW
Suite 1180
Washington, D.C. 20037
(202) 338-0111

Embassy of Saudi Arabia
601 New Hampshire Ave. NW
Washington, D.C. 20037
(202) 342-3800

Embassy of Syria
2215 Wyoming Ave. NW
Washington, D.C. 20008
(202) 232-6313

Embassy of Tunisia
1515 Massachusetts Ave. NW
Washington, D.C. 20005
(202) 862-1850

Embassy of Turkey
1714 Massachusetts Ave. NW
Washington, D.C. 20036
(202) 659-8200

Embassy of United Arab Emirates
3000 K St. NW, Suite 600
Washington, D.C. 20007
(202) 338-6500

Embassy of Yemen
2600 Virginia Ave. NW, Suite 705
Washington, D.C. 20037
(202) 965-4760

SUB-SAHARAN AFRICA

Embassy of Angola
1899 L Street NW, Suite 500
Washington, D.C. 20036
(202) 785-1156

Embassy of Benin
2737 Cathedral Ave. NW
Washington, D.C. 20008
(202) 232-6656

Embassy of Botswana
3400 International Dr. NW, Suite 7M
Washington, D.C. 20008
(202) 244-4990

Embassy of Burkina Faso
2340 Massachusetts Ave. NW
Washington, D.C. 20008
(202) 332-5577

Embassy of Burundi
2233 Wisconsin Ave. NW, Suite 212
Washington, D.C. 20007
(202) 342-2574

Embassy of Cameroon
2349 Massachusetts Ave. NW
Washington, D.C. 20008
(202) 265-8790

Embassy of Cape Verde
3415 Massachusetts Ave. NW
Washington, D.C. 20007
(202) 965-6820

Embassy of Central African Republic
1618 22nd Street NW
Washington, D.C. 20008
(202) 483-7800

Foreign Embassies In The U.S.

Embassy of Chad
2002 R Street NW
Washington, D.C. 20009
(202) 462-4009

Embassy of Comoros
336 E. 45th St., 2nd Floor
New York, NY 10017
(212) 972-8010

Embassy of Congo
4891 Colorado Ave. NW
Washington, D.C. 20011
(202) 726-5500

Embassy of Cote D'Ivoire
2424 Massachusetts Ave. NW
Washington, D.C. 20008
(202) 797-0300

Embassy of Djibouti
1156 15th St. NW, Suite 515
Washington, D.C. 20005
(202) 331-0270

Embassy of Equatorial Guinea
57 Magnolia Ave.
Vernon, NY 10553
(914) 738-9584

Embassy of Eritrea
1418 15th St., Suite 1
Washington, D.C. 20035
(202) 265-3070

Embassy of Ethiopia
2134 Kalorama Rd. NW
Washington, D.C. 20008
(202) 234-2281

Embassy of Gabon
2034 20th Street NW
Washington, D.C. 20009
(202) 797-1000

Embassy of the Gambia
1155 15th St. NW, Suite 1000
Washington, D.C. 20005
(202) 785-1399

Embassy of Ghana
3512 International Dr. NW
Washington, D.C. 20008
(202) 686-4520

Embassy of Guinea
2112 Leroy Pl. NW
Washington, D.C. 20008
(202) 483-9420

Embassy of Guinea-Bissau
918 16th St. NW, Mezz.
Washington, D.C. 20006
(202) 872-4222

Embassy of Kenya
2249 R Street NW
Washington, D.C. 20008
(202) 387-6101

Embassy of Lesotho
2511 Massachusetts Ave. NW
Washington, D.C. 20008
(202) 797-5533

Embassy of Liberia
5201 16th Street NW
Washington, D.C. 20011
(202) 723-0437

Embassy of Madagascar
2374 Massachusetts Ave. NW
Washington, D.C. 20008
(202) 265-5525

Embassy of Malawi
2408 Massachusetts Ave. NW
Washington, D.C. 20008
(202) 797-1007

Embassy of Mali
2130 R Street NW
Washington, D.C. 20008
(202) 332-2249

Embassy of Mauritania
2129 Leroy Pl. NW
Washington, D.C. 20008
(202) 232-5700

Embassy of Mauritius
4301 Connecticut Ave. NW, Suite 441
Washington, D.C. 20008
(202) 244-1491

Embassy of Mozambique
1990 M St. NW, Suite 570
Washington, D.C. 20036
(202) 293-7146

Embassy of Namibia
1605 New Hampshire Ave. NW
Washington, D.C. 20009
(202) 986-0540

Embassy of Niger
2204 R Street NW
Washington, D.C. 20008
(202) 483-4224

Embassy of Nigeria
2201 M Street NW
Washington, D.C. 20037
(202) 822-1500

Embassy of Rwanda
1714 New Hampshire Ave. NW
Washington, D.C. 20009
(202) 232-2882

Sao Tome and Principe–Contact
Permanent Mission to the UN
801 Second Ave., Suite 1504
New York, NY 10017
(212) 697-4211

Embassy of Senegal
2112 Wyoming Ave. NW
Washington, D.C. 20008
(202) 234-0540

Seychelles—Contact Permanent
Mission to the UN
820 Second Ave., Suite 900F
New York, NY 10017
(212) 687-9766

Embassy of Sierra Leone
1701 19th Street NW
Washington, D.C. 20009
(202) 939-9261

Embassy of Somalia
600 New Hampshire Ave. NW
Suite 710
Washington, D.C. 20037
(202) 333-5908

Embassy of South Africa
3051 Massachusetts Ave. NW
Washington, D.C. 20008
(202) 232-4400

Embassy of Sudan
2210 Massachusetts Ave. NW
Washington, D.C. 20008
(202) 338-8565

Embassy of Swaziland
3400 International Dr. NW
Washington, D.C. 20008
(202) 362-6683

Embassy of Tanzania
2139 R Street NW
Washington, D.C. 20008
(202) 939-6125

Embassy of Togo
2208 Massachusetts Ave. NW
Washington, D.C. 20008
(202) 234-4212

Embassy of Uganda
5909 16th Street NW
Washington, D.C. 20011
(202) 726-7100

Embassy of Zaire
1800 New Hampshire Ave. NW
Washington, D.C. 20009
(202) 234-7690

Embassy of Zambia
2419 Massachusetts Ave. NW
Washington, D.C. 20008
(202) 265-9717

Embassy of Zimbabwe
1608 New Hampshire Ave. NW
Washington, D.C. 20009
(202) 332-7100

ASIA

Embassy of Afghanistan
2341 Wyoming Ave. NW
Washington, D.C. 20008
(202) 234-3770

Embassy of Bangladesh
2201 Wisconsin Ave. NW
Washington, D.C. 20007
(202) 342-8372

Consulate of Bhutan
Two United Nations Plaza
New York, NY 10017
(212) 826-1919

Embassy of Brunei
2600 Virginia Ave. NW, Suite 300
Washington, D.C. 20037
(202) 342-0159

Embassy of China (People's Republic)
2300 Connecticut Ave. NW
Washington, D.C. 20008
(202) 328-2500

Embassy of India
2107 Massachusetts Ave. NW
Washington, D.C. 20008
(202) 939-7000

Embassy of Indonesia
2020 Massachusetts Ave. NW
Washington, D.C. 20036
(202) 775-5200

Embassy of Japan
2520 Massachusetts Ave. NW
Washington, D.C. 20008
(202) 939-6700

Korea (North)–Contact
Office of Foreign Assets Control
Department of Treasury
1331 G Street NW
Washington, D.C. 20220

Embassy of Korea (South)
2450 Massachusetts Ave. NW
Washington, D.C. 20008
(202) 939-5600

Embassy of Laos
2222 S Street NW
Washington, D.C. 20008
(202) 332-6416

Macau–Contact Portuguese Embassy

Embassy of Malaysia
2401 Massachusetts Ave. NW
Washington, D.C. 20008
(202) 328-2700

Maldives–Contact UN Mission
820 Second Ave. Suite 800C
New York, NY 10017
(212) 599-6195

Embassy of Mongolia
2833 M Street NW
Washington, D.C. 20007
(202) 333-7117

Embassy of Myanmar (Burma)
2300 S Street NW
Washington, D.C. 20008
(202) 332-9044

Embassy of Nepal
2131 Leroy Pl. NW
Washington, D.C. 20008
(202) 667-4550

Embassy of Pakistan
2315 Massachusetts Ave. NW
Washington, D.C. 20008
(202) 939-6200

Embassy of Philippines
1617 Massachusetts Ave. NW
Washington, D.C. 20036
(202) 483-1414

Embassy of Singapore
1824 R Street NW
Washington, D.C. 20009
(202) 667-7555

Embassy of Sri Lanka
2148 Wyoming Ave. NW
Washington, D.C. 20008
(202) 483-4025

Taiwan–Contact Coordination
Council for N. American Affairs
4201 Wisconsin Ave. NW
Washington, D.C. 20016
(202) 895-1800

Embassy of Thailand
2300 Kalorama Rd. NW
Washington, D.C. 20008
(202) 483-7200

Vietnam—None, but at press time Vietnam and the U.S. were in the process of establishing diplomatic posts in each other's countries.

PACIFIC

Embassy of Australia
1601 Massachusetts Ave. NW
Washington, D.C. 20036
(202) 797-3000

Cook Islands–Contact Consulate
for the Cook Islands
Kamehameha Schools #16
Kapalama Heights
Honolulu, HI 96817
(808) 847-6377

Embassy of Fiji
2233 Wisconsin Ave. NW, Suite 240
Washington, D.C. 20007
(202) 337-8320

French Polynesia–Contact
Embassy of France

Kiribati (formerly Gilbert Islands)
Contact–Embassy of United Kingdom

Embassy of Marshall Islands
2433 Massachusetts Ave. NW
Washington, D.C. 20008
(202) 234-5414

Embassy of Micronesia
1725 N Street NW
Washington, D.C. 20036
(202) 223-4383

Nauru–Contact Nauru Consulate
ADA Professional Bldg., 1st Fl.
Marine Drive
Agana, Guam, 96910
(671) 649-8300

Embassy of New Zealand
37 Observatory Circle NW
Washington, D.C. 20008
(202) 328-4800

Palau–Contact
Palau Representative's Office
444 N. Capitol St. Suite 308
Washington, D.C. 20008
(202) 624-7793

Embassy of Papua New Guinea
1615 New Hampshire Ave. NW.
3rd Floor
Washington, D.C. 20009
(202) 745-3680

Solomon Islands–Contact
Embassy of United Kingdom

Tonga–Contact Consulate
General of Tonga
360 Post St. Suite 604
San Francisco, CA 94108
(415) 781-0365

Tuvalu–Contact British Embassy or Consulate

Vanuatu–Contact British Embassy or Consulate

Western Samoa–Contact
Western Samoa UN Mission
820 2nd Ave. Suite 800
New York, NY 10017
(212) 599-6196

Appendix D

Foreign Tourist Offices In The U.S.

Many countries operate a tourist office in the United States. These offices are separate and distinct from embassies or consulates. The purpose of a tourist office is to promote travel to the country. They work with both the travel industry and the public. From a tourist office you can get a tremendous amount of free information and advice. Ask tourist offices for destination maps and brochures and for information on cities, attractions, local customs, visas, currency, weather, festivals, VAT, driving rules, hotels, restaurants, and tours. Tourist offices do not book tours; they provide information and promote tourism.

Tourist offices are a good starting point in planning your trip abroad. Here are the addresses and phone numbers of foreign tourist offices located in the U.S., listed by region.

NORTH AMERICA

Canadian Office of Tourism, 1251 Avenue of the Americas, New York, NY 10020, (212) 581-2280.
Mexican Tourism Office, 405 Park Avenue, Suite 1002, New York, NY 10022, (212) 755-7261.

SOUTH & CENTRAL AMERICA

Argentina Tourist Information, 12 W. 56th Street, New York, NY 10019, (212) 603-0443.
Belize Tourist Board, 8 Haven Avenue, Port Washington, NY 11050, (516) 944-8554/(800) 624-0686.
Bolivian Tourism, 211 E. 43rd Street #702, New York, NY 10017, (212) 687-0530.
Brazil Tourism Office, 551 5th Avenue, Suite 519, New York NY 10176, (212) 286-9600.

Chilean National Tourist Board, 510 W. Sixth St. #1204, Los Angeles, CA 90014, (213) 627-4293.
Colombian Tourist Office, 10 E. 46th Street, New York, NY 10017, (212) 949-9898.
Costa Rica Tourist Board, No office in the U.S. but you can obtain information by phone at (800) 327-7033.
Galapagos Tourism, 7800 Red Road South, S. Miami, FL 33143, (305) 665-0841.
Guatemala Tourist Office, 299 Alhambra Circle #510, Coral Gables FL 33134, (305) 442-0651/(800) 742-4529.
Honduras Tourist Office, c/o SAHSA Airlines, 360 W. 31st Street 4th Floor, New York, NY 10001, (212) 564-0378/(800) 238-4043.
Paraguay Tourism, 2400 Massachusetts Ave. NW, Washington, D.C. 20008, (202) 483-6960.
Peru–FOPTUR, 10629 N. Kendall Drive, Miami, FL 33176, (305) 279-8494/ (800) 854-0023.
Suriname Tourist, 866 UN Plaza #320, New York, NY 10017, (212) 826-0660.
Venezuelan Tourism Association, P.O. Box 3010, Sausalito, CA 94966, (415) 331-0100.

CARIBBEAN

Anguilla Tourist Office, 271 Main Street, Northport, NY 11768, (516) 261-1234.
Antigua & Barbuda Tourism, 610 5th Avenue, Suite 311, New York, NY 10020, (212) 541-4117.
Bahamas Tourist Office, 150 E. 52nd Street, 28th Floor North, New York, NY 10022, (212) 758-2777.
Barbados Tourism, 800 2nd Avenue, 17th Floor, New York, NY 10017, (212) 986-6516.
Bermuda Travel Information Center, 310 Madison Avenue, New York, NY 10017, (212) 818-9800.
Bonaire Tourist Office, 275 7th Ave., 19th Floor, New York, NY 10001, (212) 242-7707.
British Virgin Islands Tourist Board, 370 Lexington Ave., Suite 511, New York, NY 10017, (800) 835-8530.
Cayman Islands Tourism, 980 N. Michigan Ave., #1260, Chicago, IL 00611, (312) 944-5602.
Dominican Republic Tourist Information, 485 Madison Ave., New York, NY 10022, (212) 826-0750.
Grenada Tourist Office, 820 2nd Avenue, Suite 900-D, New York, NY 10017, (212) 687-9554.
Guadeloupe—See French West Indies
French West Indies Tourist Board, 610 Fifth Avenue, New York, NY 10020, (212) 757-1125.
Jamaica Tourist Board, 866 Second Avenue, New York, NY 10017, (212) 688-7650.

Martinique–See French West Indies
Netherland Antilles (Curacao) Tourist Board, 400 Madison Avenue, Suite 311, New York, NY 10017, (212) 751-8266.
St. Kitts and Nevis Tourist Office, 414 E. 75th Street, New York, NY 10021, (212) 535-1234.
St. Lucia Tourist Board, 820 2nd Avenue, Suite 900, New York, NY 10017, (212) 867-2950.
St. Martin (St. Maarten) Tourism, 275 7th Avenue, 19th Floor, New York, NY 10017, (212) 989-0000.
Trinidad & Tobago Tourism, 25 W. 43rd St., Suite 1508, New York, NY 10036, (212) 719-0540.

WESTERN EUROPE

Andorra Tourist Office, 120 East 55th Street, New York, NY 10022, (212) 688-8681.
Austrian Tourist Information Office, P.O. Box 1142, New York, NY 10108, (212) 944-6880.
Belgian Tourist Office, 780 Third Avenue #1501, New York, NY 10017, (212) 758-8130.
British Tourist Authority, 551 Fifth Avenue, Suite 701, New York, NY 10176, (800) 462-2748 or (212) 986-2200.
Denmark–Contact Scandinavian Tourist Boards.
Finland–Contact Scandinavian Tourist Boards.
French Tourist Office, 610 Fifth Avenue, New York, NY 10020, (212) 757-1125.
German National Tourist Office, 122 E. 42nd Street, 52nd Floor, New York, NY 10168, (212) 661-7200.
Greek National Tourist Organization, 645 Fifth Avenue, 5th Floor, New York, NY 10022, (212) 421-5777.
Iceland–Contact Scandinavian Tourist Boards.
Irish Tourist Board, 757 Third Avenue, New York, NY 10017, (212) 418-0800 or (800) 223-6470.
Italian Travel Office, 630 Fifth Avenue #1565, New York, NY 10111, (212) 245-4822.
Luxembourg Tourist Office, 17 Beekman Place, New York, NY 10022, (212) 935-8888.
Malta Tourist Office, 249 E. 35th Street, New York, NY 10016, (212) 213-6686.
Monaco Tourist Office, 845 Third Avenue, 19th Floor, New York, NY 10022, (212) 759-5227.
Netherlands Board of Tourism, 225 N. Michigan Avenue, Suite 326, Chicago, IL 60601, (312) 819-0300.
Northern Ireland Tourist Board, 551 Fifth Avenue, New York, NY 10176, (212) 922-0101.
Norway–Contact Scandinavian Tourist Boards.
Portuguese National Tourist Office, 590 Fifth Avenue, 4th Floor, New York, NY 10036, (212) 354-4403.

Scandinavian Tourist Boards, 655 Third Avenue, New York, NY 10017, (212) 949-2333. (Contact for information about Denmark, Finland, Iceland, Norway and Sweden.)
Spanish Tourist Office, 665 Fifth Avenue, New York, NY 10022, (212) 759-8822.
Sweden–Contact Scandinavian Tourist Boards.
Swiss National Tourist Office, 608 Fifth Avenue, New York, NY 10020, (212) 757-5944.

EASTERN EUROPE

Bulgarian Tourist Office, c/o Balkan Holidays-USA, 41 E. 42nd Street, #508, New York, NY 10017, (212) 573-5530.
Czechoslovak Travel Bureau, 10 E. 40th Street #3604, New York, NY 10016, (212) 689-9720.
Hungary Tourist Office, One Parker Plaza #1104, Fort Lee, NJ 07024, (201) 592-8585.
Polish National Tourist Office, 275 Madison Avenue, #1711, New York, NY 10016, (212) 338-9412.
Romanian National Tourist Office, 573 Third Avenue, New York, NY 10016, (212) 697-6971.
Slovenian Tourist Office, 122 E. 42nd Street #3006, New York, NY, 10168, (212) 682-5896.

RUSSIA & FORMER SOVIET UNION

Armenian Tourism, 122 C Street NW, Washington, D.C., 20001, (202) 393-5983.
Commonwealth of Independent States, Contact Intourist.
Estonia Tourism, 630 Fifth Avenue #2415, New York, NY 10111, (212) 247-1450.
Intourist, 610 Fifth Avenue #603, New York, NY 10020, (212) 757-3884.
Latvia Tourism, 4325 17th Street NW, Washington, D.C. 20011, (202) 726-6785.
Lithuania Tourism, 2622 16th Street NW, Washington, D.C. 20009, (202) 234-5860.
Russia and Former USSR, Contact Intourist.

MIDDLE EAST & NORTH AFRICA

Cyprus Tourism Organization, 13 E. 40th Street, New York, NY 10016, (212) 683-5280.
Egyptian Tourist Authority, 630 Fifth Avenue #1706, New York, NY 10111, (212) 332-2570.
Israel Government Tourist Office, 350 Fifth Avenue, New York, NY 10118, (212) 560-0600.

Jordan Information Bureau, 2319 Wyoming Avenue NW, Washington, D.C. 20008, (202) 265-1606.
Moroccan National Tourist Office, 20 E. 46th Street #1201, New York, NY 10017, (212) 557-2520.
Saudi Arabia Tourism, 866 UN Plaza #480, New York, NY 10017, (212) 752-2740.
Tunisia Embassy Tourist Section, 1515 Massachusetts Avenue NW, Washington, D.C. 20005, (202) 862-1850.
Turkish Tourism Information Office, 821 UN Plaza, New York, NY 10017, (212) 687-2194.

SUB-SAHARAN AFRICA

African Travel Association, 347 Fifth Avenue #610, New York, NY 10016, (212) 447-1926.
Cote D'Ivoire Tourism, 2424 Massachusetts Avenue NW, Washington, D.C. 20008, (202) 797-0344.
Gabon Tourist Information Office, 347 Fifth Avenue #810, New York, NY 10016, (212) 447-6701.
Gambia National Tourist Office, 347 Fifth Avenue #610, New York, NY 10016.
Kenya Tourist Office, 424 Madison Avenue, New York, NY, 10017, (212) 486-1300.
Malawi Tourism, 600 Third Avenue, New York, NY 10016, (212) 949-0180.
Mali Tourism, 111 E. 69th Street, New York, NY 10021, (212) 737-4150.
Mauritius Government Tourist Information, 8 Haven Avenue, Port Washington, NY 11050, (516) 944-3763.
Nigeria Tourist, 828 Second Avenue, New York, NY 10017, (212) 808-0301.
Senegal Tourist Office, 888 Seventh Avenue, 27th Floor, New York, NY 10106, (212) 757-7115.
Seychelles Tourist Office, 820 Second Avenue #900F, New York, NY 10017, (212) 687-9766.
South African Tourism, 500 Fifth Avenue, 20th Floor, New York NY, 10110, (212) 730-2929.
Tanzania Tourism, 205 E. 42nd Street #1300, New York, NY 10017, (212) 972-9160.
Uganda Tourism, 336 E. 45th Street, New York, NY 10017, (212) 949-0110.
Zambia Tourist Office, 237 E. 52nd Street, New York, NY 10022, (212) 308-2155.
Zimbabwe Tourist Office, 1270 Avenue of the Americas #412, New York, NY 10020, (212) 332-1090.

ASIA

Bhutan Travel Inc., 120 E. 56 Street #1130, New York, NY 10022, (212) 838-6382.
Burma, see Myanmar.

China National Tourist Office, 60 E. 42nd Street #3126, New York, NY 10165, (212) 867-0271.
Hong Kong Tourist Association, 590 Fifth Avenue, 5th Floor, New York, NY 10036, (212) 869-5008.
India Government Tourist Office, 30 Rockefeller Plaza, 15 N. Mezzanine, New York, NY 10112, (212) 586-4901.
Indonesian Tourist Promotion Office, 5 E. 68th Street, New York, NY 10021, (212) 879-0600.
Japan National Tourist Office, 630 Fifth Avenue #2101, New York, NY 10111, (212) 757-5640.
Korea National Tourism Corporation, 2 Executive Drive, 7th Floor, Fort Lee, NJ 07024, (201) 585-0909.
Macau Tourist Information Bureau, 70A Greenwich Avenue #316, New York, NY 10011, (212) 206-6828.
Malaysian Tourist Information Center, 818 W. Seventh Street #804, Los Angeles, CA 90017, (213) 689-9702.
Myanmar (Burma) Tourist Agency, 10 E. 77th Street, New York, NY 10021, (212) 535-1310.
Pakistan Tourism, 12 E. 65th Street, New York, NY 10021, (212) 879-5800.
Philippine Department of Tourism, 556 Fifth Avenue, New York, NY 10036, (212) 575-7915.
Singapore Tourist Promotion Board, 590 Fifth Avenue, 12th Floor, New York, NY 10036, (212) 302-4861.
Sri Lanka Tourist, 2148 Wyoming Avenue NW, Washington, D.C. 20008, (202) 483-4025.
Taiwan Visitors Association, One World Trade Center #7953, New York, NY 10048, (212) 466-0691.
Thailand Tourism Authority, 5 World Trade Center, #3443, New York, NY 10048, (212) 432-0433.

PACIFIC

Australian Tourist Commission, 489 Fifth Avenue, 31st Floor, New York, NY 10017, (212) 687-6300.
Cook Islands Tourist Authority, 6033 W. Century Blvd. #690, Los Angeles, CA 90045, (310) 216-2872.
New Zealand Tourism Office, 501 Santa Monica Blvd. #300, Santa Monica, CA 90401, (310) 395-7480 or (800) 388-5494.
Papua New Guinea Information Office, c/o Air Niugini, 5000 Birch St. #3000, Newport Beach, CA 92660, (714) 752-5440.
Tahiti Tourism Board, 300 N. Continental Blvd. #180, El Segundo, CA 90245, (310) 414-8484.
Vanuatu National Tourism Office, 520 Monterey Drive, Rio del Mar, CA 95003, (408) 685-8901.

Appendix E

International Measurements

As soon as you enter most countries, you will encounter a new system of measurement. Most of the world measures weight and distance by the metric system and temperature by the Celsius (or centigrade) system. You will be more comfortable if you have an understanding of the U.S. equivalents of the metric and temperature measurements used abroad.

Distance
1 centimeter = .39 inch
1 meter = 39.4 inches, or 3.3 feet, or 1.09 yards
One meter is 3 inches longer than a yard

1 inch = 2.54 centimeters
1 foot = 30.48 centimeters
1 yard = .91 meters

1 kilometer = .62 miles
1 mile = 1.6 kilometers
To figure the number of miles from kilometers, multiply the kilometers by 0.6.
Example: 48 miles is 28.8 kilometers. (48 x .6 = 28.8)

Weights
1 gram = .04 ounce
1 kilogram = 2.2 pounds
1 pound = .45 kilograms

Liquid Measure
1 liter = .26 gallons
1 Imperial gallon = 1.2 U.S. gallons
1 U.S. gallon = 3.79 liters
1 U.S. quart = .95 liters

When buying gasoline a useful shorthand conversion is that 4 liters is a little more than 1 U.S. gallon.

Temperature
The Celsius scale uses 0°C for the freezing point of water (32° in Fahrenheit) and 100° for the boiling point of water (212° in Fahrenheit). To convert Celsius temperatures into Fahrenheit, multiply the Celsius temperature by 1.8 and then add 32.
Example: A Celsius temperature of 12° is 53.6° in Fahrenheit. (12 x 1.8 = 21.6 + 32 = 53.6)

Index

A

Agricultural products, importing 133–136
  Canadian products 135
  fruits & vegetables 133
  information 136
  meat & animal products 133
  Mexican products 135–136
  permissible products 134–136
  plants 133
  soil & sand 134
AIDS. *See* Diseases, AIDS
Alcohol, foreign entry prohibitions 39
Allergies 86
American Automobile Association
  foreign affiliates 58–59
  International Driving Permits 60
  maps 60
  traveler's checks 51
American consuls. *See* Consuls, U.S.
American Express
  mail hold service 62
  money transfer 55
  traveler's checks 51
Animal & Plant Health Inspection Service 107–108, 131–138
Animals, importing 131–132
Antiques, bringing into U.S. 129–130
APHIS. *See* Animal & Plant Health Inspection Service
Arriving in countries. *See* Entering countries
Art, bringing into U.S. 129

ATMs 54, 76
  safeguarding withdrawals 76
Auto insurance abroad 59
Automatic teller machines. *See* ATMs

B

Birds, pet, bringing into U.S. 132–133
Blood transfusions abroad 96–97
Books, bringing into U.S. 126–127
Bureau of Alcohol, Tobacco and Firearms 128

C

California use tax 123
Cash
  carrying abroad 52
  safeguarding 76
Cats, bringing into U.S. 132
Centers for Disease Control 94, 132
Certificate of Registration 120
Cholera. *See* Diseases, cholera
Citizens Emergency Center 48, 79, 87
Collision damage waiver 59
Computer programs, bringing into U.S. 126
Consular Affairs Bulletin Board 79
Consular Information Sheets 71, 78–80
Consular officers. *See* Consuls, U.S.
Consulates general, U.S. 43. *See also* Embassies, U.S.

Index 179

locations 141–157
Consulates, U.S. 43. *See also* Embassies, U.S.
  locations 141–157
Consuls, U.S. 44, 71
Contact lenses 86
Country Entry Requirements 21–36
  Asia 33–35
  Caribbean 24–26
  Eastern Europe 28–29
  Middle East & Northern Africa 30–31
  North America 22
  Russia & Former Soviet Union 29
  South & Central America 22–24
  Sub-Saharan Africa 31–33
  Western Europe 27–28
Country information, obtaining 70–71
Credit cards
  acceptance abroad 53
  converting charges to U.S. funds 53
  traveler's assistance programs 68, 86–87
Cruise ship sanitation 106
Customs, foreign countries 38
Customs Service, U.S. 107–108, 111–124
Customs, U.S.
  California use tax 123
  Certificate of Registration 120
  Customs assistance 111–124
  customs declaration 111–112
  duty exemptions 113–115
  exemption levels 113–115
  gifts 121
  GSP duty exemptions 117–120
  mailing & shipping to U.S. 121–122
  packing bags for inspection 123
  payment of duty 117
  personal belongings taken abroad 120
  proving values 123
  rates of duty 115–117

D

Departing countries 41–42
  customs 41
  export restrictions 41–42
  immigration 41
Department of State. *See* State Department
Departure taxes 42
Disease risks 89–90
Diseases 89–94, 95–106
  after traveling abroad 106
  AIDS 95–96
  cholera 91–92
  food borne 102
  insect borne 97–99
  malaria 99–100
  mosquito borne 97–99
  schistosomiasis 105
  travelers' diarrhea 103–104
  water borne 101–102
  yellow fever 90–91
Dogs, bringing into U.S. 132
Driver's licenses 60
Driving abroad 58–60
  AAA services abroad 58
  gasoline prices 58
  injury risks 105–106
  road tax 58
  safety 75–76
Drug violations 73
Duty-free shops 125–126

E

Embassies, foreign, U.S. locations 158–169

Embassies, U.S. 43
  locations 141–157
  medical care, help finding 86
  services not provided 47–48
  services provided 45–47
    death abroad 46–47
    destitute travelers 45
    disasters or evacuations 46
    emergency messages 45–46
    jail visits 46
    medical assistance 45
    non-emergencies 47
    replace passport 45
    when to register with 44
Endangered species souvenirs 136–138
Entering countries 37–41
  currency 40
  customs processing 38–39
  immigration 38
  prohibited items 39
Entry/exit forms 38
ETS. *See* Value Added Tax
Eye glasses 86

F

Fake articles, bringing into U.S. 125
Federal inspection fee 108
Firearms
  bringing into U.S. 128
  entering foreign countries 40, 73–74
Food and Drug Administration 128
Foreign currency 49–51
  black markets 50, 76
  currency restrictions 49–50
  exchanging 50–51, 52
  hard currencies 49
  soft currencies 49
Formal entry 122

G

General Services Admin., travel information 82
Generalized System of Preferences. *See* GSP duty exemptions
Glazed ceramics, purchasing abroad 129
Gold, bringing into U.S. 128
Goods & Services Tax. *See* Value Added Tax
Govt. Printing Office, travel information from 80–82
GSP duty exemptions 117–120
  eligible countries 119–120
  eligible products 117–119
GST. *See* Value Added Tax

H

Health insurance abroad 66–67
Hearing aids 86
HIV virus. *See* Diseases, AIDS

I

IAMAT 87
Immigration processing, foreign countries 38
Immigration processing, U.S. 109–110
Immigration Service, U.S. 107–108
Immunizations 89–94
  cholera 91–92
  disease outbreaks 92
  information 93–94
  recommended 92–94
  required for travel 90–92
  to return to U.S. 92
  yellow fever 90
Inoculations. *See* Immunizations
Insect repellents 98–99

Index   181

Insurance
   auto coverage 59
   health 66, 87–88
   travel 66–69
International Certificate of Vaccination 91, 93
International Driving Permit 60
International measurements 176–177
Intnl. Assoc. for Medical Assistance to Travelers. *See* IAMAT

L

Local laws 73

M

Mail
   par avion 61
   Poste Restante 62
   receiving while abroad 62–63
   sending from abroad 61–62
Malaria. *See* Diseases, malaria
Malaria information 100
Map Link 60
Map sources 60
Medic Alert Foundation 86
Medical care, locating 86–87
Medical coverage abroad 87–88
Medical evacuation 67, 88
Medical kit 86
Medicare coverage abroad 66, 87
Medicine
   bringing into U.S. 127–128
   carrying abroad 73, 85–86
Money
   bringing large sums into U.S. 126
   safeguarding 76
   taking large sums out of U.S. 52
   transferring from U.S. 55
Most Favored Nation Status 115

N

Narcotics, bringing into U.S. 127–128

O

Onward/return ticket 21, 40–41

P

Packing precautions 72
Par avion 61
Passport waiver fee 6
Passports 5–14
   additional visa pages 11
   children 6
   defined 5
   denied or revoked 13
   fees 9
   for family members 6
   how to apply 6
      by mail 10–14
      in emergencies 10
      in person 7
   loss or theft 11
   name change 11
   Passport Agencies 13–14
   photographs 9
   purpose 5
   second passports for visas 12
Permanent resident aliens 5
Pets
   bringing into U.S. 131–133
   entering foreign countries 40
Photography restrictions 74
Pickpockets 74
Post offices, foreign 62
Post travel illnesses 106
Poste Restante 62
Prescription drugs 73, 85–86
   bringing into U.S. 127–128
   carrying abroad 73, 85–86
Proof of sufficient funds 21

R

Recordings, bringing into U.S. 126
Resident consular agents, locations 141–157
Return ticket/onward ticket 21, 40
Ruesch International 51

S

Safety abroad 70–77
  driving 75–76, 105–106
  hotels 75
  money & valuables 76
  public places 74
  public transportation 75
Schistosomiasis. *See* Diseases, schistosomiasis
Shells, bringing into U.S. 134
Shots. *See* Immunizations
State Department
  help for travelers 43–48
State Department travel information, 78–82
  automated fax system 79
  computer information services 79
  Consular Affairs Bulletin Board 79
  Consular Information Sheets 71, 78–80
  Travel Warnings 71, 79–80
Summary of Health Information for Intnl. Travel 93
Swimming, disease risks 105

T

Telephones abroad 63–65
  Dial U.S. direct programs 64–65
  hotel surcharges 63–64
Terrorism 77
Tourist cards 20

Tourist offices, foreign, U.S. locations 170–175
Trademarked items, bringing into U.S. 130
Travel Advisories. *See* Travel Warnings
Travel insurance 66–69
  medical coverage 67
  nonmedical coverage 67
  sources 68–69
Travel Warnings 71, 79–80
Traveler's assistance programs 67
Traveler's checks 51
  foreign denomination 51
  safeguarding 76
Travelers' diarrhea 103–104
Traveler's health clinics 93

U

U.S. citizenship, proving 109–110
U.S. Fish & Wildlife Service 138
Uniform Stamp 91

V

Vaccinations. *See* Immunizations
Value Added Tax (VAT) 55–57
  Europe Tax Free Shopping (ETS) 56
  Goods & Services Tax (GST) 57
  refunds 56–57
Videos, bringing into U.S. 126
Visa denials 19
Visa services 17
Visa violations 19
Visas 15–20
  costs 15
  country entry requirements 21–36
  extension of stays 20
  obtaining 16
  travel agents 17

types 16
when needed 16

W

Water, treating 101–102
Western Union, money transfer 55
Wildlife, importing restrictions 136–138
  coral reefs 138
  furs 137
  ivory 137
  plants 137
  reptile products 137–138
  wild bird products 137–138
World Wildlife Fund 138

Y

Yellow Card. *See* International Certificate of Vaccination
Yellow fever. *See* Diseases, yellow fever

Ordering Information

Please support your local bookstore. If you are unable to obtain a copy of *The International Traveler's Handbook* from your bookstore, single copies may be ordered directly from the publisher. Send $13.95 plus $1.75 for shipping for each book ordered. Washington State residents please add sales tax. Send orders to Farwest Publishing, P.O. Box 1340, Issaquah, WA 98027. For phone inquiries call (206) 392-6177. Contact the publisher for quantity discount information.